Legacy Lit
Hachette Book Group
1290 Avenue of the Americas
New York, NY 10104
LegacyLitBooks.com
@LegacyLitBooks
First Edition: April 2024

Legacy Lit is an imprint of Grand Central Publishing. The Legacy Lit name and logo are registered trademarks of Hachette Book Group, Inc.

The publisher is not responsible for websites (or their content) that are not owned by the publisher.

The Hachette Speakers Bureau provides a wide range of authors for speaking events. To find out more, go to hachettespeakersbureau.com or email HachetteSpeakers@hbgusa.com.

Legacy Lit books may be purchased in bulk for business, educational, or promotional use. For information, please contact your local bookseller or the Hachette Book Group Special Markets Department at special.markets@hbgusa.com.

Print book interior design by Marie Mundaca

Library of Congress Cataloging-in-Publication Data
Names: Dyer, Deesha, author.
Title: Undiplomatic : how my attitude created the best kind of trouble / Deesha Dyer.
Description: First edition. | New York : Legacy Lit, [2024]
Identifiers: LCCN 2023052353 | ISBN 9781538741696 (hardcover) | ISBN 9781538741719 (ebook)
Subjects: LCSH: Dyer, Deesha. | United States. White House Office—Officials and employees—Biography | Imposter phenomenon. | Success.
Classification: LCC E901.1.D94 A3 2024 | DDC 973.93092 [B]—dc23/eng/20240108
LC record available at https://lccn.loc.gov/2023052353

ISBNs: 9781538741696 (hardcover), 9781538741719 (ebook)

Printed in Canada

MRQ

Printing 1, 2024

For the ones who call me Aunt or Auntie, especially Justice, Jasmyne, and Bam. May you forever hold tight to your curiosity and wonder, never questioning your worth, brilliance, beauty, and place in this wide adventurous world. You are loved.

And they asked me—who do you think you are?
With a wide-toothed grin, I boldly whispered...
everything.

CONTENTS

INTRODUCTION

I'm going to work at the White House."
    "The store?"

Fifteen years after this conversation happened with my cousin, I still break out in uncontrollable laughter. She, like I, was in complete disbelief when I received news of my acceptance into the White House Internship Program, nine months into the Obama presidency and just a few months shy of my thirty-second birthday. Although I would have completely worn out the employee discount code at the White House Black Market clothing store, I was indeed referring to the mansion behind the iron gates that take up the 1600 block of Pennsylvania Avenue in Washington, DC. What followed was eight years of a journey I could never have planned or predicted, one full of joy and unexpectedness, one that encompassed almost my entire thirties and left me every day asking, often without answer, why me? One quick look at my life trajectory and it was obvious I had no business being in anyone's White House.

This book answers that question, a testimony of sorts that weaves heavily through a well-fought and well-won battle with chronic imposter syndrome. A battle that started way before I stepped into politics, it was planted from childhood, through boarding school and multiple college attempts. Whether I am speaking at esteemed institutions, corporate boardrooms, academia, or community organizations, my message about the messy, oppressive, and often mishandled world of imposter syndrome ends with a triumphant victory dance that lies in the details of my story. But writing about it all is challenging and it's important for me to briefly touch on the why for you, the reader.

Let's start briefly at the beginning, shall we? *Imposter syndrome* is a term that was coined the same year as my birth, 1978! Isn't that a coincidence?! It was the brainchild of two women psychologists and used to speak to this phenomenon of successful women who felt like frauds in professional spaces despite all they had achieved. Over time, the term has taken on a life of its own and become a brand that put the ownership on women (and others who are treated like their lives don't matter), making it seem like either they were being delusional or they had the power to change their inner feelings of doubt by analyzing, correcting, or controlling their own actions. This in essence is a sham, a scam, a genius move. It ignores the impact and hold that systems have on us by redefining behaviors of sexism, racism, classism, homophobia, ableism, etc., as imposter syndrome. It's truly a trickery of the mind that has transcended to people from all walks of life, especially those who have been historically oppressed and discounted in our society. Who says we aren't qualified? Who says we aren't as good as the next person, aren't deserving and worth all the promotions, accolades, and good things that happen to us? Like, really, who? This was all such a mystery for me and knowing this didn't immediately erase the deeply embedded conditioning. I used to be embarrassed that it took so long to come to the reality that I've been duped into believing it was always me and my problem to solve, when truthfully I just had to cut the puppet strings. That's easier said than done. I get it.

Reader, it does no good for me to write this book in the present voice and present body in which I have come out on the other side, because truthfully that isn't where many of you are right now. In these pages, I will meet you in the uncomfortableness of trying to figure it all out, while also taking you on a wild ride. I'm more about walking beside than ahead. I wasn't prepared for the pain of writing about my former self, as my current self. It was hard to not default or backslide to that person who would've wondered why anyone would want to read about her life or the person who compares herself to bestselling authors who dominate the market on vulnerability, confidence, and, frankly, politics. I write this from the space and frame of mind of who I used to be, which allows you to witness this evolution in real time. I am your example, your motivation, and your inspiration to know that there is space to breathe. Just hold on.

While a large chunk of this book takes place at the White House, a fancy, shiny, jeweled space, I want to emphasize that achievements, especially those that come with an elite imagery and grave importance, are not required for you to have access to a space of internal freedom. Accomplishments are lovely and can serve as a catalyst to knowing you are deserving, but the high we experience from them isn't always permanent, so we must be careful of using them as a foundation of our worth.

In storytelling there is a power that transforms, humanizes, connects, and helps us feel less alone, no matter what we are going through. We all deserve to live and speak our truths with the manner in which we lived them. May the burden you put down today give room for the joy, curiosity, courage, and love that you will pick up tomorrow.

If you are one of those who has always stood tall with your shoulders back and felt confident in who you are, I encourage you to take these words and tell them to those who aren't quite there yet. If anything, please enjoy the tales of fabulous events, epic world travels, global diplomacy, and one, two, or three all-night dance parties.

And by the way…does anyone have a White House Black Market discount code?

CHAPTER 1

Hey, Imposter. Nice to Meet Ya?!

One June night in 2009, I was cooking dinner and my rottweiler, Change, was lazily watching me as I stirred meat sauce for spaghetti, waiting for a drop to casually fall into his lap. My microbraids were pushed up under my bed bonnet already on my head for the night and to keep them off my sweaty neck. I could not let my hair absorb the delicious onion, tomato, and garlic smell of the food. Jill Scott and Mos Def were serenading my ears with the "Love Rain" remix, a track off Jilly from Philly's debut album, which I'd listened to weekly since it came out in 2000. The song has a vibe of hip-hop, soul, and jazz blends with lyrics that rise above the beat just perfectly.

Love rain down on me, on me—down on me.

My hips subtly swayed on this hot Philadelphia day. My apartment was steaming and had a window air-conditioner unit that sort of worked when I sealed the cardboard down on the side with sturdy duct tape and prayed that it stayed put through the night. The music stopped abruptly. I looked at my phone and saw a call coming in from an unidentified number.

It was after 8:00 p.m. and I was in my groove. If your credit is funny like mine, you know very well that this could be a bill collector, so answering the phone is at your own risk. The best options are to ignore or answer in a different persona. Putting on my best white-woman professional voice, I answered "Hello?" into my new, sleek iPhone 3G, not knowing that this call would change the course of my life.

On the other end was the wholesome voice of a twenty-something. He said that he was calling from the Office of Scheduling and Advance to interview me for the fall White House Internship Program.

"Um, okay?" I said, throwing down the spoon full of sauce on a pot holder I grabbed from the oven door. I was whipping up enough pasta to last for the next few days, so I'd have no reason to turn on the stove again in the oppressive heat. I turned the knob to OFF and lightly placed all the dirty cooking dishes in the sink with soap and water so Change wouldn't use his big paw to knock them off the counter and enjoy the fruits of my labor. I was frazzled and filled with nervous anxiety because this all felt like an out-of-body experience.

Patrick was following up on an application I'd

submitted two months before to be a White House intern. I had no idea what the Office of Scheduling and Advance did, but he explained that it handled and supported President Obama's daily schedule and all travel. As he dove deeper into the mechanics of the department, I scurried around the apartment for something to write with. I grabbed a pen and an old piece of junk mail and started jotting down as much as I could, still not quite knowing whether this was a formality of the application or whether I had gotten an internship. A steady stream of *okays* poured from my mouth robotically to let him know I was cool, calm, and paying attention—but my heart pounded in my ears. He apologized for going on so long about the department and then spoke words I will never forget: "We are interested in interviewing you to be a fall intern."

I moved from the kitchen to my bedroom, where it was quiet. I sat down on the bed, staring out the window to the row house next door as Patrick continued telling me the terms of the internship. Change followed me, still hoping he'd get droppings from dinner. "Thank you. I am very interested," I said, silently leaping off the bed so excitedly that Change started barking.

I was thirty-one years old, on my second attempt at college after a failed first attempt at seventeen. I now had only twelve college credits to my name. I'm not even sure exactly what made me think I would actually be chosen. I had an eviction on my record and terrible credit, I'd written about a past abortion in the newspaper, and I didn't have any connections to politics—unlike some, who'd been active in government since college or had family members who held positions in Washington. There was no political legacy in my bloodline or lifeline, which as it turned out was a good thing.

I had a résumé full of unexpected detours. I hadn't applied for the internship in the hope that I'd get it, but I'd been curious enough to try.

I grew up on the East Coast, only two and a half hours from Washington, DC. Even though it wasn't a huge distance, the nation's capital felt far away. In my school we'd studied a sanitized version of American history that just included past presidents, the founding fathers, and the three branches of the government. I'd learned about Black people like Shirley Chisholm and Thurgood Marshall only because one of the two Black teachers in my primary school taught history. In middle school, we watched the *Schoolhouse Rock!* episode that explained how legislative bills worked through a rolled-up-paper cartoon, aptly named Bill—singing "I'm just a bill. Yes, I'm only a bill" while hopping around Capitol Hill with a sunken face looking for support to be introduced as a law.

I was lost and confused as to why anyone would want to make a career in politics. When I had the chance to vote in my first election, in 1996, I had no idea how it all worked and how, ultimately, something called the Electoral College decided who occupied the Oval Office.

This all changed when a Black man from Illinois found notoriety in the Democratic Party and, shortly thereafter, the world. He went by the name Barack Hussein Obama.

Although he was already a junior senator giving infectious and impactful speeches that had both Black and white America gripped with wonder, I didn't know this man. In my mind, it wasn't a possibility that a Black man could become president of these United States, because we'd never had one before, and, well, racism, oppression, slavery. Pick one or all three. As he declared his candidacy in 2007, I thought, *How cute, his hope gave him permission to dream the impossible dream*, but I figured he'd eventually have to wake up to the reality that there was no way in hell this could or would happen. But like many others, I became engaged in the election *because* of him. He spoke about issues that were important to me, like economic disparities, criminal justice reform, healthcare, and lack of opportunities and access for Black youth; he knew how to interact with veteran politicians and curmudgeons steeped in traditions of old, while also two-stepping and preaching his way into the homes of Black people. He had a nontraditional background that I identified with and a family that included a beautiful Black wife, Michelle Obama, and two daughters who had press & curls, platts, and Afro puffs.

Senator Obama's golden touch was joyful and euphoric, stern but relatable. By the time the election rolled around in 2008, I'd watched this hope and change movement sweep the world. I sat on the sidelines, wanting in like a high school freshman on a varsity bench, but school plus three jobs kept me from having time to volunteer, so I scrounged up a few dollars and sent it to the campaign almost monthly. I'm talking about $10. In return, I received a thank-you letter from Barack Obama, which I was so geeked about. I didn't know back then that he didn't personally write it or sign it!

When he did exactly what I thought he couldn't do—win the presidency on November 4, 2008—Philadelphia was energized. Black radio stations set up tents around the voting locations with DJs playing the classics like "Ain't No Stopping Us Now" by McFadden & Whitehead, "Respect" by Aretha Franklin, and what felt like Stevie Wonder's entire catalog. That night, our city soundtrack was a mix of honking cars, drums, cheers, screams, hugs, and, of course, music, as people flooded the streets to celebrate the historic victory. I wanted to freeze in time these moments that felt like we were all on the highest of highs.

My then-boyfriend and I gleefully ran out of our apartment on foot and landed on 52nd Street, the epicenter of West Philly life. On our way there, we passed more than a dozen street vendors selling Obama bootleg everything—shirts, hats, glow necklaces, framed photos of the family, and more. Black folks were smiling ear to ear with genuine happiness over the history that just unfolded. As we marched down the street hugging complete strangers, it started to drizzle. But no one cared, not even me with my relaxed hair that I knew would kink up in the rain. The neighborhood crowded into a local restaurant at 52nd and Spruce to watch the president-elect give a riveting acceptance speech in Chicago's Grant Park.

"And to all those watching tonight from beyond our shores—from parliaments and palaces to those who are huddled around radios in the forgotten corners of our world—our stories are singular, but our destiny is shared."

The election year was busy for me for other reasons. In addition to being a student, I held several jobs, including a nine-to-five at a real estate company as the secretary to the chief accounting officer. It was my first time having a salaried job with benefits. While I wasn't interested in real estate, this job paid the bills. I got it through a staffing agency that I contacted once I moved back to Philadelphia from Cincinnati in 2001. At the same time, I worked at a youth center and an engraving shop in a mall, and I became a permanent fixture on the hip-hop scene covering the local culture for a website and later a newspaper.

Writing was always my creative outlet. In tenth grade, we were tasked with writing about our future. It had to be handwritten and fifty pages long. It was an easy assignment for me. I loved writing as much as I loved hip-hop. Growing up in the 1990s, I gravitated toward the elements of hip-hop culture—not just the music, but the graffiti, breakdancing, and DJing. I repeatedly watched the movies *Wild Style* and *Beat Street*, which came out when I was six and seven, respectively. I started to copy the moves of the dancers and gave myself the culture name Vibin' when I was in middle school. I'd scribble it on notepads at school like I was practicing to tag a wall. I was just a fan having fun with a mediocre hand, though my dancing continued to evolve. I remember watching the Fly Girls perform on the '90s comedy show *In Living Color*. I recorded every episode of the show to play over and over practicing their dances. It led me to a very short stint of dancing behind hip-hop groups at festivals and concerts. It was a good time—an avenue I wasn't good enough to pursue professionally, nor did I want to, but it deepened my involvement in the culture. I was there to witness cyphers and open mics at places in Philly like the Five Spot, which saw an array of soul superstars rotate weekly—Erykah Badu, Kindred the Family Soul, Bilal. I watched the careers of Philly legends like Eve, Freeway, and Bahamadia take off. It was beyond a vibe, it was a family—a gritty style of brotherly love and sisterly affection.

When a friend started a website focused on Philly hip-hop talent, I boldly suggested I write a column called *Vibin' with Deesha*, where I'd interview those in front of and behind the scenes. It was casual, unedited, and didn't follow a cadence, style guide, or formality. I got paid absolutely nothing, but I loved it. I would grab people before or after an event, ask a series of random, corny questions—what was their favorite cereal, the cliché question of when they fell in love with hip-hop—and then write up the answers. I loved it and over time,

I became a freelancer for various outlets, expanding my content to other genres, festivals, and community events. I did this for nine years and enjoyed documenting through photos and words this beautiful culture that transcended borders around the world. Hip-hop and all its art forms were foundational to everything I touched.

It inspired me to found an initiative called Cover Your Lover, which expanded my existing work in the AIDS community. I focused on reducing the number of HIV transmissions by handing out condoms, dental dams, and testing information at hip-hop concerts. My nickname became "the Condom Queen." At this point, I'd seen more than I wanted to see backstage, so I would make a special protection packet for the artists and either throw it onstage or give it to them if we had an interview scheduled. Looking back, I'm unsure how I had the energy or bandwidth to do all of this. I was unknowingly searching for purpose, while also doing my best to stay afloat financially.

Leading up to the presidential election, I'd thumbtacked a photo of Senator Obama that I'd ripped from the front of a magazine to my dark-gray cubicle, so that everyone who came by my desk would know where my allegiance stood. It was also a joke toward my boss, Jon, who never stated he was a Republican, but had recently received a signed thank-you photo of party nominees John McCain and Sarah Palin in the mail.

"When Obama becomes president, I'm going to leave here and go work for him," I jokingly told my boss. "Okay, we'll see," he responded. We laughed it off and I went back to my desk. The political climate of 2008 was a bit different than now. I had worked for Jon for nearly six years, and this was the first time we'd uttered a sentence about politics. Although we had a great working relationship—I knew his wife, kids, and Social Security number, and I'd even been to his home—we didn't discuss current affairs, news, or our viewpoints on elections. Our business was real estate and finance. It was often a dry environment that lacked controversy or color. I was good at being Jon's secretary and doing what I needed to do to keep my job. I answered phones, managed calendars, prepared him for important meetings, filed papers, and typed up financial reports. I wasn't quiet but I wasn't loud. I quickly made friends with the other Black women who worked there, who by chance were also mainly secretaries. We'd go to lunch together and discuss our personal lives, things like kids and relationships, but also commiserate over our jobs. Back then, political discourse didn't dominate every facet of our lives, but when the Black folks from my job got together we'd express our joy and anticipation over having a Black president. We discussed how it would make so many white men, our bosses, cringe a bit. The thought made us giggle.

"I told Jon I was going to work for Barack Obama when he becomes president," I mentioned to co-workers as we were heading down to eat lunch in the food court of our building.

"He would miss you, but wouldn't that be something," Giana said. Upon arriving at the food court, we changed subjects and got our sandwiches. I proceeded back upstairs to eat at my desk and do homework as I often did during my hour lunch break. Before opening up my literature book and personal laptop, I ran back the conversation about going to work at the White House.

How does that actually happen? I wondered. *Do they put jobs in the classified section? What normal person without connections actually works there?* I had a lot of questions and absolutely no answers. It was all hypothetical anyway. Lord knows, no one was hiring someone without a college degree to work with the president of the United States.

Inauguration 2009 came and went. The first Black president and his family were all moved into 1600 Pennsylvania Avenue. What a joy it was to watch him take the oath at the Capitol, walk the streets with his wife and kids, and walk into the White House where they would live for eight years. I threw a celebratory brunch on that frigid day in January. Friends came over wearing unofficial Obama apparel they bought from the street vendors as we toasted and cheered inside our living room over themed food items like Hillary hash browns, Obama orange juice, Go Back to Texas toast & jelly, Biden bacon, and my favorite, Michelle mimosas. So corny, but also so funny.

As winter turned into spring, the high of President Obama's election lingered, but life also started to return to normal and my grind of juggling multiple jobs, school, volunteering, and writing recommenced. I went back to not caring so much about the political news and paid attention only when the president or First Lady was doing an interview or giving a speech. Since the election was over, I took the magazine cover of Obama down in my cubicle, figuring I'd rubbed it in my boss's face enough. Unrealistic, silly me didn't want to give up the far-fetched vision of working for Obama, but I had to be for real.

One day, several months after the election, I was wasting time at work and checking my personal email. I saw an email from an AOL jobs and opportunities list-serv I was subscribed to that read, "Apply Now for the White House Internship Fall Program." The opportunity was sent to me as part of a group of community leaders who worked with young people interested in public service or politics. My initial reaction was to do what I'd done with many of these emails—forward it to everyone in my address book, so they could pass it on, especially to Black students. I was so excited to log on to Facebook and post the details. How amazing would it be if I was the one who found a White House intern from Philly? As I started to craft the email and draft the posts, I googled *internship* because I only had a very loose idea what it actually was.

Surprisingly, the list of qualifications didn't seem that bad. Well, not as hard as they should be for the White House. College, desire and passion for community and civic service, an essay, a résumé, and letters of recommendation—that was it? A weird feeling came over me suddenly—*could I possibly apply for this?* Seemed a little too easy, so I dug deeper. Every single article or blog I read about internships mentioned that they are for college students who are pursuing a bachelor's degree in a particular field; the internship would be at a company or organization that specialized in that field. I gathered that "college students" meant those who are nineteen through twenty-three, so I combed the details in the fine print looking for the bubble-burst of an age restriction. It wasn't there. This was a crazy idea.

I again combed through the application for language about a bachelor's degree requirement, thinking *This will be it, the reason I can't apply.*

I couldn't find it.

I then *again* skimmed the requirements looking for college majors like political science or international relations as must-haves. I was a women's and gender studies major. Surely, that'd be it, the nail in the coffin of why I couldn't apply.

It wasn't there.

I started to talk myself out of applying. I gave myself reasons why I wasn't qualified and why I wouldn't be the right candidate for this prestigious opportunity. I told myself, *This isn't for me. They are looking for someone better, more polished. I haven't earned this.* Then I realized that I had absolutely nothing to lose by trying. That email was never forwarded, and I never advertised it on Facebook.

I was going for it myself. My excitement grew as fast as my doubt. The two voices argued back and forth in my head. I anonymously joined a message board of White House intern hopefuls who had been preparing their applications for weeks. They identified themselves by their colleges—Princeton, Howard, Spelman,

UCLA, and Penn State were among the ranks. Scrolling down the screen, I didn't see one community college represented. But maybe there was a community college student hiding, like me. I left the school name in my profile blank. I wasn't ashamed of getting my associate's degree; I was just afraid that I'd come across as less smart than everyone else.

Reading over hundreds of posts, my mind played tricks on me by the minute. One minute I felt confident: I could compete with these kids by writing an explosive essay on something cutting-edge, relevant, and hip. The next minute, they all seemed custom-groomed for this internship, with their big words, in-step majors, and impressive colleges. My feelings of inadequacy grew as I read posts where people talked openly about their application essays. All the conversations were the same—policy, policy, policy. Unfortunately (or fortunately) for me, I didn't know much about that. *Policy* just wasn't a term I used regularly, or ever. I read over the message board's tips for the required essay. It made me feel both dumb and motivated. Dumb in the sense that every essay sounded like it followed the same formula: lots of really elongated words that didn't make sense to an everyday person. I honestly needed to stop and look up some of them in a dictionary. I couldn't fake the funk, though, and decided to create an essay focused on what I was passionate about and what I knew—how we could spark change by loosening power, giving freely of resources and funds. I reminded myself that the Barack Obama who'd won the election did so by doing just that. I still was a dreamer.

Since I did most of my studying during my lunch break and late at night after dinner, I reserved 5:00 p.m., right after work, to craft my essay. Often after everyone went home from work for the day, I'd hole myself up in the large conference room, which was located five floors beneath me. There I pieced together scattered Post-it notes with my ideas about the essay, which I'd scribble down throughout the day as they came to me.

I won't lie, though. As I was putting together this paper, I went back and forth in my head about what those in Washington would want to read about—what would make me seem smarter, make me seem anything but a thirty-one-year-old college dropout. I had just watched a news report about the one-child policy in China and thought, *Well, maybe I should write about that.* But what did I know besides what I'd just learned on TV? I quickly scratched that idea and brainstormed further on what I could write about quickly, but passionately and directly.

The result was a well-crafted piece that spoke to how the country can use music and the arts in general to more effectively teach students in city schools, specifically concentrated on hip-hop culture. Although other applicants seemed born for this internship, I knew I could compete in writing. None of that fleeting confidence killed my feelings of inadequacy, though, so I decided to delete my message board account to eliminate distractions and comparisons. I prepared myself for the soft landing of rejection.

I spent the next two to three weeks perfecting my application. I went over it more times than I could count, checking grammar and punctuation, swapping out the Philly slang I was used to like *jawn* and *bol*. I glanced over my school transcript on my screen, hoping my 3.6 GPA would override the fact that it was from a community college. When answering the question of why I wanted this internship, I stated that, like going back to school, applying for a White House internship was something I would never have imagined myself doing, but I'd been inspired by Barack Obama and there was no time like the present. I closed with, "As the country enters a new era with its first Black president, I am moved to help actualize what this means for people everywhere." That was the first time I'd used the word *actualize*. I sounded so professional and I loved it.

The application also asked us to choose the top ten White House departments that we'd want to intern in, out of about fifteen. Some departments, like the Oval Office, were hiring only one or two people, while others, like Correspondence, were looking for twenty to thirty. The Office of Public Engagement and Intergovernmental Affairs seemed to me to most closely work with the community, so that was my first option. I followed it with the Domestic Policy Council and, third, the Office of the First Lady, because who wouldn't want to work with Michelle Obama? I randomly ranked the rest based on the loose description we were given. I listed Scheduling and Advance as number eight, two up from the bottom of the list.

After dissecting the entire application for what seemed like the millionth time, I filled in fun questions about my favorite song ("Closer" by Goapele) and favorite sports team (Philadelphia Phillies—who, by the way, had just won the World Series). On the day the application was due, I stayed at work late to eliminate any temptation to plop and chill in front of the TV. I printed the application out and read over everything one last time. All the lights were out except my overhead lamp. The cleaning supervisor, Vaughn, whom I'd gotten to know pretty well, poked his head around the corner: "You need anything to eat?" Since I kept a few frozen meals at work for busy-workday lunches (Lean Cuisine raviolis were my favorite and cheap), I'd used one of those for dinner. "No, thank you."

I felt a sense of power being there alone. There was no one asking me to get the phone, type up papers, or arrange a department lunch, as secretaries do. Although I was sitting at my work desk, I felt like a different person. I felt heavy with tempered expectations but light with infinite hope. It was just me, this application, and a gallon of sweet iced tea from Rite Aid. Feeling as good as I could about the submission, I hit SEND at 9:22 p.m., a little under three hours before the deadline. Even if I'd wasted my time, I was proud. Proud that I tried.

The weeks immediately following were freeing. Applying marked an important milestone in my life—a moment when I had worked through self-doubt, self-imposed deficits, age insecurity, education insecurity, and all the life mistakes I'd put up as roadblocks. What happened next was no longer up to me, I told myself. I even stopped obsessively checking my phone and refreshing my email. But as weeks went by, I let any small glimmer of hope I had for the internship fade. When you have imposter syndrome, you psych yourself out of opportunities. Either you act like you don't care when you really do, or you convince yourself you won't get the opportunity anyway so that the impending failure won't hit as hard. I was used to this, and as the weeks swept by, I did both.

Maybe I'd been riding Obama's idealistic wave a little too long, to the point where it'd left me delusional. That wave had helped me and the world actualize a Black man as president, but maybe that was as far as it was taking me. That, I felt, was the one miracle out of all of this, though I still felt sadness. I ruminated over how my application could have been better and how, if I'd done everything like everyone else—four years of college, master's, law school, business school—maybe then I would have aced this opportunity, and I would have heard from the White House by now. I beat myself up for everything I couldn't change.

Two months went by with nothing more than a communication acknowledging and thanking me for my application. It was one of those automated emails that everyone receives.

Until the phone rang that hot July night while I was making spaghetti.

After the initial shock of the White House actually being interested in me had passed, as I sat there in my apartment with my rottweiler staring up at me and the smells of my food still wafting from the kitchen, I learned that Patrick was actually calling me to schedule a time for an interview, which would be with him. It was after working hours already, so not the ideal time for an interview, but I was afraid to let this chance go. What if, between now and then, he forgot about me, or they found another amazing candidate?

I told Patrick that it was no problem to just do the interview now, if he had time. My adrenaline was pumping, and my excitement could only propel me with added confidence through an interview right then and there. He agreed to just go ahead and conduct the interview on that same call and proceeded to ask questions that centered on my ability and experience with office work—spreadsheets, filing, typing, and those basics. He asked about situations in which I'd had to use discretion and keep things confidential. And he spent most of the time asking me about my writing skills, stressing that interns in his department help respond to constituent requests for the president to attend various events and meetings. I talked to him in detail—maybe a bit too much—about my freelance career, which I'd been in for seven years at this point.

When I hung up the phone, I felt good. I knew that I'd answered every question to the best of my ability, coming across as poised, experienced, hungry (both in ambition and appetite, since I hadn't eaten yet), and excited. It was a familiar feeling—one I'd had on election night. I felt unstoppable, and although we were supposed to keep the details of the interview private, I immediately called a few close friends, specifically so that they could pray for me.

I had burned part of the dinner and didn't have any energy to cook anything else, so I ordered a cheesesteak with onions, peppers, and ketchup from a neighborhood spot, Accu Pizza, around the corner. I started eating it on my way home from picking it up, and as I peeled the foil from the bread to take my first bite, I felt my cheeks smile at the thought that I'd just talked to the White House. I went to bed with a slight stomachache from scarfing down my sandwich but I was on top of the world.

That feeling, however, was very short-lived as the voice of uncertainty soon found its way back to my body and made a nesting place to hibernate. It was telling me that once Patrick started digging into my background, he'd find out that I wasn't who they were looking for. He would realize that I presented good on paper and good in the interview, but not good enough.

The wait commenced.

I started to emotionally pull out from the whole process. I stopped talking about the internship and would answer every inquiry from friends about it with, "I haven't heard anything, so I didn't get it." I assumed that because, at this point, the internship started in about a month. (I mean, it was the White House, so they were rightfully busy and couldn't email me back. Fine, I get it.)

Weeks after my late-evening interview, my phone rang again. On the other end was the FBI. Yes, that FBI—the Federal Bureau of Investigation. They were looking for the security forms that had been sent to my email two weeks before to start the White House internship process! The voice sounded like a standard government worker reading off a script bored, going from call to call chasing down irresponsible students for paperwork. As I quickly opened up my computer to look for the email that he said had been sent weeks ago, the voice on the other end politely agreed to resend the forms. I kept digging through my digital trash and archives for the acceptance email while thanking the worker over and over again. I couldn't catch my breath. There was a moment of shock, panic that butted up against my excitement and disbelief. I hung up and just froze in my chair for a split second before screaming and calling my best friend Kerri in Ohio to tell her the story.

And there it was.

The email he referenced had looked more like spam than official government business (not that I even knew what "official government business" emails looked like), and I had deleted it without even reading! Yes, that's right—straight to the black hole of Gmail. Maybe I'd deleted it without reading it because, in my mind, I'd already lost the internship. Maybe it was a self-fulfilling prophecy, subconscious self-sabotage.

But wait, what was happening? I WAS GOING TO BE A WHITE HOUSE INTERN and I had only a month to get ready!

Everything became blurry. A time warp of sorts where the minutes of each day meshed together. I filled out my SF-86, a twenty-five-plus-page security form, which I was unsure I'd actually pass because it asked about everything from your drug history to your credit to disclosing anything that the US government would deem *unsavory*. I informed all my jobs, school, and volunteer organizations that I would be taking a break for three months. Then I had to figure out how I was going to actually live off this unpaid internship with very little savings and no place to stay in DC. I started to count up all my coins, hoping I had enough to rent a place for three months and eat. The internship paid for our transportation to work, so thank God for that! But they had a very strict policy against us holding other jobs, though they would make exceptions if necessary—since the internship was unpaid. I also had to discontinue writing, as the White House wasn't keen on me freelancing while I was there.

I applied for night and weekend jobs in DC at gyms, cafés, grocery stores, practically everywhere. I scoured Craigslist to look for a room to rent and found one in Southeast DC with a married couple that was headed to divorce. They still lived there with their younger daughter; I'd be renting the room that had previously been occupied by their older daughter, now at college. It was messy as hell most days, but also very cheap.

I didn't own a blazer or proper work pants, so I scoured department stores for acceptable clothes and bought one black blazer, three shirts, and two pairs of pants. I packed a small U-Haul and drove down to DC with a twin bed, one basic TV, a DVD player, and the entire boxed set of the show *The West Wing* that someone had lent me. I wouldn't have cable and had never seen the show, but countless people insisted I needed to watch it and tell them if working at the White House was just like it was portrayed on TV.

A few days before I left, my co-workers organized a fundraiser for me. On my last working day before I left Washington, my day job surprised me with $4,000 and a send-off party. I'd been very honest with them about how difficult it was going to be without a salary, but I'd never expected them to do something so generous.

After the party subsided, Diane, the secretary for the CEO, Ralph, called me into his large corner office, where he wanted to see me. I had a good relationship with Ralph but I also could count on two hands the number of times I had been in his office in eight years. He had dark, comfortable furniture, including a wooden desk with family photos. I nervously sat down in one of the expensive but squeaky chairs. Diane was standing in the room near the back as Ralph handed me an envelope. He instructed me to open it later but said, "I hope this helps you enjoy your time in Washington a bit more. Good luck. We are rooting for you." I politely thanked him while Diane escorted me to the elevator and gave me a hug. "We're gonna miss you around here." My plan was to come back, as they were holding my job and allowed me to keep my health benefits while I was gone. With a box on my hip and my purse on my shoulder, I walked out of the downtown Philly building and hopped in a taxicab out front, as I wasn't carrying that box on public transportation. As soon as I got in the cab,

I opened up the envelope. It was a substantial check, one big enough to help me through the internship and beyond. I teared up in the cab with disbelief.

All good things were happening, and while I was doing my best to live in these moments, I spent time questioning why *I* was afforded this opportunity. I made excuses upon excuses. This was all happening so fast, and I didn't feel deserving. Instead of praising and thanking God, I asked him why me and not someone else. I had a hard time digesting that it wasn't luck and that no one had made this happen for me. *I* did this. *I* actually did this.

I met a few of my fellow interns online before our first day. They were all current students from nineteen to twenty-two who attended four-year public and private schools across the country. There were a few in graduate school. Some had worked on the presidential campaign at their colleges and some were already involved in politics through family members. We all agreed to meet on the first day outside the White House at 17th and Pennsylvania, where one of the four visitor gates is located. I was convinced it would be painfully obvious that I was the intern in my thirties who'd never owned a business suit and had gone to community college. I even wore fake glasses in the hope of appearing smarter, more studious. I did everything I could to prove I belonged there, even if internally, I wasn't quite sure. This feeling enveloped me before I even stepped foot inside the iron gate, which was guarded by more than four officers from the Secret Service. Since I didn't have a driver's license, I handed them my passport through a small opening in a glass-shielded window—the kind of windows that we have at the corner stores in Philly, if you know what I mean. I stood there nervously and for a minute went through over a dozen scenarios that all ended with them telling me to go home.

Instead, they ushered me into the Eisenhower Executive Office Building, adjacent to the White House and West Wing. I moved slowly up never-ending gray cement stairs. With each step, I was able to see more and more of the executive mansion. It was stark white and much smaller than I imagined. Every few seconds, a black sedan would pull up on West Executive Avenue, which sat outside the West Wing, and someone in a navy or black suit, with a briefcase in one hand and a BlackBerry in the other, would rush from the car and walk swiftly into the building. With each car, I gasped in the hope that President Obama would be in the next car to pull up—*after all, the man does live here*—but it was morning, so he wouldn't be commuting in a car to work.

I settled into the South Court Auditorium, which had about two hundred seats and a stage set up lecture-style. There were an estimated 120 or so interns, who were all freshed, dressed like a million bucks. I wore a black, oversize blazer I'd bought from Ross Dress for Less for $15 that I'd matched with a pair of straight-legged dark khaki-like pants. I had my hair in long braids, like the ones Janet Jackson rocked in the movie *Poetic Justice*. I didn't know if anyone else would have braids, but I also wanted something easy since I'd be away from my Philly hairdresser for a few months. And I wasn't trusting any new stylist in DC to relax and trim my hair.

I made a conscious choice to find the Black interns, specifically the women, and befriended them all pretty fast. They reminded me of home, and we reminded each other that we all were there for a reason, even if we didn't know what that was.

I specifically connected with Chanel, a vibrant, excited, energetic young woman from Oakland, and Alisha, a native of Detroit who was tall, beautiful, and serious about her business! She lived in Nashville with her husband and recently finished a master's program. They became my Black girl magic crew. We'd often meet up for lunch or go to intern events on campus together. The three of us were fairly new to DC so we'd do things on the weekends like go to museums and festivals. Alisha found out she was pregnant during our internship, and we threw her a mini baby shower with a few other close interns we got to know. Since Alisha and I were both older than Chanel, we became her big sisters, often dishing out career and man advice. We always looked out for one another. One time when I didn't understand how to do formulas in Microsoft Excel and felt so dumb that it was truly laughable, I called Alisha, who was just in the office next door. I'd spent years using Excel as a secretary but for some reason this particular project was hard. She rushed over to calm my fears of looking like an idiot to my supervisor while helping me. These two and a few others always helped me through.

Imposter syndrome went to the White House with me. When I got the internship, so did it. It will always show up on time for your accomplishments. It will become your best friend and sometimes your only friend.

I can't pinpoint the exact reason why I took a chance on me and applied for the internship. I guess I wanted to know if I could actually do it, if I could actually do something so prestigious and competitive, if I could be on the same playing field as those we hold up as successful. I proved that I could, that it was possible. But I walked into the experience giving it the heavy responsibility of fixing my confidence issues and reversing what I thought about myself—that the route I'd taken in life was wrong because it wasn't traditional; that it was the result of bad decisions I'd made. I wanted to walk out of the White House and be ready to conquer the world, use it to level up my status in a judgmental society where what you do matters more than who you are. I was chasing the high of achievement to erase the imposter syndrome, not realizing that the lack of self-worth that lies dormant inside of so many of us can't be deleted by the momentary high of achieving a goal. It does for a minute, yes, but then the exhaustion sets in as we try to keep up. Accomplishments can be motivation, but when you depend on them, it can become an addiction to always compete, compare, and be perfect—all in a quest to find your value.

I wasn't what I'd call the ideal candidate, but I was the right one. Too often we get in our heads about all the ways in which we don't fit in or aren't qualified. We make up narratives based on past experiences. We normalize and vocalize doubt in ourselves and our abilities to the point that it becomes our identity, instead of a temporary obstacle. There's a lack of compassion when we do that, a silencing of the voice that tells us it's all going to be okay. In those moments, any type of positive light will be hard to see, but all the while testimony is brewing. I didn't know then how much my life would change after the fall of 2009, or how much I would change. But I knew nothing would ever be the same.

CHAPTER 2

Digging Up the Root

I was nine years old when my mother dropped my brother and me off at Milton Hershey School (MHS) in Hershey, Pennsylvania, in 1987. The private boarding school was for children from financially struggling families, created against a backdrop of chocolate, farms, and the kind of rural scenery you'd find on country store postcards. As we got closer to the school, we could smell a potent mix of cocoa beans and cow manure. The manicured lawns and bushes of the campus sat underneath silver lampposts in the shape of Hershey kisses. I strained my neck looking out the window as we passed Hersheypark. My eyes grew big at the sight of the amusement park's roller coasters, which cascaded over the trees. I had never been to Disney World, but I imagined that Hershey, Pennsylvania, was pretty darn close. I was familiar with Milton Hershey School through my cousin, who was a few years older than me and had been a student there several years before I arrived. He would come home to Philadelphia during the holidays and summers and tell us of his adventures being a Milt (the nickname for students who attended MHS).

Growing up, I was conscious that we had less money than others, but I didn't see it as a problem. We moved from Philadelphia to Warren, Ohio, when I was seven, and once that happened I didn't see my cousin as much but continued to get updates about his time in Hershey. My parents were divorced, and my dad lived in Philadelphia. In Ohio, we stayed with distant relatives. I remember once sleeping with a pillow and blanket on those plastic beach lounge chairs that were popular in the 1980s—the ones that went the whole way back lying flat. I had seen them used often on television shows where ladies in their stylish bathing suits would be lying on a beach in lounge chairs folded all the way down, working on their tans. I loved the show *Three's Company*, and I wanted to visit San Diego, where it was filmed, so I could lie on the beach with Janet, Jack, and Chrissy. All I could think about was how my family was sleeping in luxury like the fancy folks on TV. I didn't think about the fact that we didn't have actual beds at the time.

I started elementary school in Ohio. I loved my school and the new set of friends that I'd walk to school with daily. My brother had his own crew and walked in another direction to the junior high school. We were latchkey kids, meeting up back at our house after school to supervise ourselves until our mom returned from work. We'd eat dinner together, which was usually a heavy rotation of spaghetti, eggs, hot dog and beans, and chicken.

As school was winding down for the year, my mother let us know we would soon be heading to join our cousin at Milton Hershey School. I don't remember feeling any emotions. I don't remember what happened between her telling us and us arriving in Hershey in 1987. But I do remember being scared. Although I'd have my brother in Hershey with me, we weren't going to be living in the same house. I wouldn't have my mother there, either. I'd be placed in a home with thirteen to fifteen other girls my age and watched over by houseparents, adults who were in charge of our well-being and day-to-day life. I don't remember my dad being there when we arrived in Hershey, and I didn't understand at the time that it was a school for poor kids.

Once we passed the amusement park, streetlights, gazebos, and chocolate factory, we pulled into a very large building called Founders Hall that sits in the center of the MHS campus. We got out of the car with a bag of belongings and proceeded inside to be greeted by a bunch of adults whom I interpreted as big, scary strangers who were taking me away from my family. My mom kept assuring us it was going to be okay and that she was just a phone call away before hugging us and going into a separate room with other parents who were dropping their kids off that day. There were five of us in the room. We all just looked at one another with skepticism and confusion. My brother and I were the only siblings present. I was so relieved he was there. He was a familiar face and would be a protector in the everyday absence of my mom.

We watched basic videos before being told to say goodbye to our parents. The videos painted a whole-some view of the school, showing children playing, laughing, and having fun around campus. I was still scared, but my sadness started to ease up when the students appeared happy. I hugged my mom and my brother before getting in a van and being taken to stu-dent home Elmwood, which would become my home from fifth through eighth grades. I walked in with my four-foot-nothing frame, head hanging low and skittish body language. For as sassy as I always was, I didn't want to talk. I met the rest of the girls, some who had been in Milton Hershey since kindergarten. They were all different races, ethnicities, and ages. I met my houseparents, the Martins, who were so bubbly and welcomed me with a big hug. They were a white couple who reminded me of people who'd be on *Ses-ame Street*—so wholesome, innocent, and dedicated to children. I could picture them right away hosting sing-alongs, taking us apple picking, and playing in the snow while also being sure we dressed properly, always said grace before meals, and remembered our manners in public and private. I didn't know them, but felt okay enough in their presence to not have a total meltdown being left with strangers. The Martins had two biolog-ical children who lived at Elmwood with them in the houseparent quarters, which were under the same roof as us but separate. Their daughter came out to say hello. She was a bit younger than me and had a French braid.

Maybe they could braid my hair like my mom.

I was shown my room, introduced to my roommate, and given a tour of the house. Everything was so organized. I had never seen anything like it. Each girl had her own cubby in a tall wooden closet for clean laundry, and we had hooks and bins in the basement for outside shoes and raincoats. Every single room in this place was spotless. There were perfectly parallel lines in the rug from the vacuum and sectional sofas large enough to fit all the girls on them in the front of the TV. I saw three bathrooms upstairs and three downstairs, where there were also three showers. I was so overwhelmed, but also really excited to get to meet all these new friends who would eventually become like sisters. As we were walking past the rooms, I saw twin beds all made the same with corners: a sheet and blanket tucked at a ninety-degree angle under the mattress. There were stuffed animals and blankets on top of the beds, while right above was a wall cluttered with thumbtack posters from magazines of teenage heartthrobs like New Edition, Al B. Sure, Jon Bon Jovi, and even Michael J. Fox. I heard music as I passed some rooms and lit up when I recognized Madonna's "La Isla Bonita" playing.

Beautiful faces, no cares in this world.

The song helped me feel settled. I loved it so much and played it every day at home on my Walkman. I twisted my neck hard to see who was playing it.

"Hiiiiiii," the girl said from her desk when she saw me staring. She looked older than me and I later found out she was an eighth grader. I was embarrassed she'd caught me and scurried away like a mouse to catch up to my houseparents, who were waiting for me at the end of the long hallway.

After the tour, I was taken to a place called the Clothing Room. I climbed the stairs and saw rows and rows and rows of clothes, shoes, and toiletries. Another woman, who was very broad and tall, introduced herself and told me she'd be taking my measurements. I sat in silence and turned to the left and to the right as commanded. She wrote down some numbers on a form that was attached to a wooden clipboard. I had a bag of clothes I'd brought with me from home and figured I'd just wear and wash those all year. My favorites were outfits that I'd picked out with my mom. I quickly found out that the Clothing Room was called that because there you were given all-new clothes that fit the standard of what we were expected to wear and how we were expected to look. I also found out later that some kids came to Milton Hershey with no clothes, so the Clothing Room was providing some with regular outfits for the first time in their short lives.

I was escorted through racks of clothes categorized by garment type. The Clothing Room lady, as I began to call her, gave me a specific number of articles of clothing that I was to have in my wardrobe. It was the same number everyone had and included pants, skirts, dresses, and shirts, all categorized into house clothes, play clothes, and school clothes. I got undergarments and pajamas, house shoes, and an outfit called Sunday Best, which we were required to wear to the weekly church service—a church dress with lace and a collar, black dress shoes, pantyhose/nylons, and a London Fog trench coat that I drowned in so much, I felt like Inspector Gadget hiding tools in the pockets. She then handed me toiletries like a comb, brush, toothbrush, and toothpaste. I asked for soap and lotion, which she told me I would get at the student home. I wasn't quite at the age when getting new clothes was fun, so I was really just confused by the whole process. I was also upset that I wouldn't be allowed to wear my Lisa Lisa & Cult Jam T-shirt to school. It was my favorite shirt that I'd brought from back home.

I got back to my student home and was taken through my chore responsibilities—vacuuming the hallway, living room, and dining room. My schedule included waking up at 6:30 a.m. to do chores, have breakfast, and get ready for school. In Elmwood, you got to sleep in a little bit longer based on your chores or grade. The eighth graders woke up twenty minutes after us, and we made sure we were already showered and out of their way by then. Then we'd all walk to school in the morning together.

My houseparents explained the disciplinary system to me and how my chores and room would be evaluated daily. If either wasn't satisfactory, I would be docked points, which could add up to equal a very large chore, like cleaning the kitchen after meals or doing laundry by myself. This wouldn't be so bad if it was a normal house-hold, but with sixteen girls plus the houseparents and their personal family, it'd total twenty people to clean up after.

As I settled in, I learned that between all of this, I could giggle with my new friends, talk, flip through magazines, swap tapes in our Walkmans, and gossip about middle school drama, which usually included which one of us got a note from a boy that day or who got asked to be someone's girlfriend. We laughed until our set bedtime, which was usually around 9:00 p.m. Maybe this all wouldn't be so bad, I thought. Just maybe.

Milton Hershey School became my warped and blissful reality for eight years. One that my young brain couldn't fully comprehend then, but has started to fully process now as a healing adult. MHS was its own world. We did everything together and didn't interact much with the world outside of the picturesque bubble that we ultimately grew to call home. So many situa-tions and circumstances that shape our identities, ide-ologies, and foundations happen from our formative to adult years, and my life was heavily influenced by a place that didn't reflect the world in which we grew up. MHS gave me the beautiful tolerance and need to be in constant community with people who shared hard life circumstances enough to uplift, encourage, and create joy for one another. These are lessons I will never for-get. Ones I carry with me as I continue to understand how my confidence was directly affected by being in a space that didn't make room for individuality and culture, instead pushing us all through the same filter of exceptionalism that wasn't always accessible or attainable. I experienced criticism around my appearance and a few attempts to straighten my kinky 4c hair; I wasn't given Vaseline or good-quality lotion for my skin; my loud voice was translated as aggressive, leading people to believe I was a delinquent insubordinate. For as much as I loved MHS, the people I met and the immediate safe environment it provided me in middle school, I had to confront the reality that it also deepened my insecurities. Puberty and adolescence also didn't help the matter. Leaving Elmwood and the loving care of the Martins, who raised me all through middle school, was hard. It was again leaving a familiar space, like I had four years prior when I came to MHS.

Despite my okay grades and involvement in activities like color guard, softball, track, and volunteering at the shelter in the neighboring city of Harrisburg, I was very quickly labeled by teachers and administrators as a troublemaker who always talked back, defied authority, and didn't follow rules. Our school wasn't small, and I'd hear repetitive comments about my behavior from teachers I didn't even have in class.

Your attitude needs to be fixed.

You're mouthy.

You'll get nowhere acting like that.

You'll be lucky to graduate.

I should fail you because of your attitude.

I wasn't the only one. There was always a gang of misfits at Milton Hershey who were on the edge of getting kicked out. Now, I'm not saying I never, ever deserved to be reprimanded, but even when I was justified in speaking up or I wasn't saying anything at all, the reputation that followed me was that I was a hard one to handle. I remember getting in trouble over things as basic as my dress shoes at church in high school. I didn't want to walk down the steep aisle in church because we wore heels. This was during a choir performance, where we entered from the back singing and continued to the stage. I wasn't coordinated enough to sing and walk in heels down the aisle. God forbid I'd fall and embarrass myself in front of my friends. So I didn't wear the shoes, instead opting for sneakers so I wouldn't fall. This set off a shitstorm at my school. I was called a delinquent and told that "my constant defiance would not be tolerated." I was given the punishment of 30/30—thirty days of detention after school and thirty hours of labor. I was even prescribed antidepressants after this to control my roller coaster of emotions and mood swings, which I was told was the cause of my outbursts. After feeling like a zombie for three days on Zoloft, I figured out how to hide the pills under my tongue as my houseparents watched me take them. I spat them out immediately after they walked away. And my labor was cleaning the wrestling mats after the team's practice as the athletes watched. I was told I needed to be humiliated as discipline.

From ninth to twelfth grade, I was moved among five student homes as they tried to figure out what to do with me. It honestly broke me a bit and started me questioning everything about myself like why I was never good enough.

I almost had my high school diploma pulled thirty days before graduation for alleged abuse of a teacher stemming from the shoe incident. I'd never been abusive in my short life, but after I got in trouble for not wearing the right shoes in church, the disciplinarian of our school came to pull me out of class to let me know what a mess I'd caused and how I'd be dealt with properly. I responded with a casual and sarcastic, "Okay," went back into the classroom, and shut the door. She was still standing there as I went unbothered back into class. The door hit her in the face, and she claimed I abused her. It was threatened that my diploma would be withheld until I sought psychiatric care, which ended up getting cut short because my grandmother came to a meeting with my mom about my behavior and let them know how ridiculous an abuse claim sounded. She put on her church-deacon voice, decibels raised with each word: "You should be ashamed of yourselves to say you have Christian values, treating a child like this." I had not seen Mom Mom like that often, especially outside of church—but she put the fear of God in them that day.

I was led to believe that everything I had growing up in Hershey was solely because of luck—not because I was deserving of an alternative, stable environment and a good education. I was lucky to have a roof over my head, lucky to have food on the table, lucky to go to a boarding school, lucky to have clothes and shoes.

It made me feel indebted to the givers of these gifts.

I believed that I owed someone for my survival. Seeds of imposter syndrome were watered heavily in me at Milton Hershey School, and the roots would grow into twisted vines that clung to the walls of every part of me for decades to come. This is a painful and vulnerable space to be with a place that I am supposed to love so much. As if gratitude and criticism can't live in the same space, as if the hard and bad parts don't hold as much merit as the good ones. They matter and hold weight in who I turned out to be.

When I sought therapy as an adult, my therapist, Dr. G, would often ask me about my childhood, as most therapists do. I zipped past all the starter-kit beginning details like family structure, relationship history, the major ups and downs of my life, and my professional/personal balance, hoping we'd get to the part where she'd give me homework, I'd complete it, and voilà, I'd suddenly be the most confident person in the world able to walk upright and believe that I could do anything. I found out rather quickly that that's not exactly how therapy works! Dr. G kept speaking about my inner child, which, frankly, sounded absolutely loony to me as an adult. How do you talk to the young version of yourself, or even identify with childlike feelings, when you haven't been a child for a very long time?

She kept asking me to go back to the time when I went to Milton Hershey, what it felt like, and what my emotions were back then. I thought to myself, *Like, lady, I don't remember how I felt. I was nine years old.* After two months of sessions, just as I was about to quit because I wasn't seeing instant results, I had an unexpected break-through. She cited examples where I may have lost a little bit of innocence, protection, trust, and wonder. As she began to equate the loss of safety and belonging to current situations I was going through and how they made me feel, a sliver of understanding opened in me. I was always looking for safety, belonging, and validation because these things eluded me growing up, to the point that I felt I didn't deserve them. It was, oddly, starting to make sense to me why I lacked confidence or constantly felt like an imposter—and this is before I had the self-awareness to understand how my Blackness was weaponized to play on my feeling of inferiority. My therapist had me focus on times I felt carefree as a child—when I was full of excitement and joy visiting my cousins in New York, running after the ice cream truck at my grandmother's house in North Philly before coming inside to listen to a TV show on radio (my grandmother didn't have a TV), holidays with my whole family, playing in the yard with my brother, or taking occasional trips with my dad to the Jersey Shore. As she dug in further each session, I started to feel a safety net to surrender in. I'd gotten used to walking on eggshells out of fear of being hurt, being yelled at, punished, and ridiculed. This bled into my sense of confidence, often tainting my ability to feel secure in who I was. I didn't have the privilege of safety, so when it finally found me, it embraced me in the best way possible, in the way I wanted and needed.

I was tasked with making a list of memories from

childhood through adulthood and attaching emotions and ages to them. We'd start off the session with writing the new ones down on a flip chart to discuss. I started to see the connections between experiences of varying ages and repeated emotions—cycles that were automatically repeating with different situations and scenarios as I got older or entered a new job, relationship, or environment. I was, in essence, digging up the root of my issues.

Oh, this was so much harder for me than it sounds. I am a procrastinator in all realms and facets of my life, and getting help isn't any different. Simply going to therapy wasn't enough; actually *engaging* in therapy was what helped me. There's never an issue with me talking about things, but actively listening, being uncomfortable, and applying the work I learned inside a session to my everyday life was hard. It continues to be hard to this day as I pull up more roots, uncovering and exposing more connections that lead to healing.

Part of uncovering these roots was acknowledging the mask that I formed at Milton Hershey School. It was a mask I took with me after I graduated. I carried it everywhere, making sure to push away my authentic self in fear that who I was wasn't enough. I learned to present well with this mask so that people would like me, jobs would promote me, and I would get praise for assimilating. I shrank myself in rooms, keeping my head down and trying not to be noticed, pushing through things without complaint. This was all so exhausting, but it is what I learned would bring me success. This is what I had to endure, especially in the eyes of those who sat in places to influence my future—those in the upper class and in executive positions. I wanted to impress them, and for a time, I wore a mask to do just that. But it never felt right. I felt suffocated trying to be someone I knew I wasn't—and then in the end still thinking I wasn't whole. It gets tiring not believing that you are good enough. You warp yourself into someone else hoping that version of you is accepted. I learned how to do this as a child, and until therapy I didn't realize that the lessons I'd digested then were now fully formed habits, a kind of operating manual for how I carried out life. When I realized this—when *we* realize this—compassion for our inner child forms, softening the harsh reality that we've been living a life that says we must earn our space in this world.

Accepting the truth that I didn't need to do this was my first step to a true freedom. It woke a powerful version of me that is no longer hiding behind a mask in fear or shame.

I'm not that child anymore, and neither are you.

CHAPTER 3

College: As Seen on TV

Being an '80s baby definitely had its perks. Technically, I was born in 1978, but those first few formative years don't really count, as I have no recollection of life before age three. Before heading to Milton Hershey School, I was part of the generation where it was pretty normal for my brother and me to go to a neighbor's house after school without weeks of arranging back and forth. Even though it was a rotating one, I always had a village. In addition to my neighbors, there were my grandparents and trusted friends of my parents who sometimes looked after us after school until my mother came home from work or we were old enough to look after ourselves. I enjoyed childhood—laughing and playing, digging in the dirt for worms, playing with my Cabbage Patch dolls, swapping charms on my necklaces and scrounging up whatever coins I found around the house to buy my favorite penny candy at the market, Swedish fish. The store clerk watched us closely to make sure we didn't take one piece too many. If we had a dime, we were getting only ten pieces of candy. Sneaking extra meant being banned from the market and, even worse, facing the wrath of our parents, who would shrill with embarrassment at the thought of us stealing.

As I got older, I discovered the "stories," what we (Black folks) call the soap operas. I started rushing to the market for candy, but instead of playing until the lights came on outside, I parked my butt down in front of the TV for the star-studded ABC lineup: *Ryan's Hope, One Life to Live,* and *General Hospital.* I had no business watching any of these grown-people shows, but I was invested. My upstairs neighbor Gail would tape the earlier ones for me to watch after school.

Television became an escape. I never wanted to be an actor, but I always imagined myself in the opening scenes, dancing to some catchy theme and then flashing a coy smile at the camera when my name was highlighted. Just like those bratty-looking kids from the Mickey Mouse Club. Being a TV star seemed like the best thing, the furthest thing, something that was reserved for people in another world—not for me.

Facts of Life was the first theme song I remember memorizing. "You take the good, you take the bad, you take them both and there you have the facts of life, the facts of life." Tootie was the only Black character on the show, and I desperately wanted to be Tootie. There weren't a lot of Black people on the shows I watched, like *Mama's Family*, *Perfect Strangers*, *Golden Girls*, and *Family Ties*, but I got that fix from *The Jeffersons*, *Good Times*, *Sanford & Son*, and *Amen*. I just thought there were Black shows and there were white shows—and what a delight that I got to watch both. In many ways, television helped raise me. It wasn't until later that I realized the Black shows were all steeped in being poor or overcoming struggle or some type of social justice element that my six-year-old brain couldn't quite comprehend.

In 1985, I discovered *The Cosby Show* and my world completely changed. This was a show about an upper-class Black family whose kids never seemed to be worried about penny candy or meals. They were wholesome and fun, and their house had several sets of stairs, plus countless bedrooms *and* bathrooms. Each parent came home after their job as a doctor and a lawyer. The kids didn't sit in front of the TV watching stories with neighbors and relatives. This show was different. I became so obsessed that my grandfather would tape each episode for me to rewatch every week. He was also very proud to see a wealthy Black family on TV. I'd sit on the edge of his bed, carefully ordering the episodes by their VCR tape label, highlighting the ones that contained my favorites, which were always the singing/dancing episodes. I memorized the choreography from the "Night and Day" episode that the Huxtables performed for their grandparents, including a baby Rudy lip-syncing, "Baby. Baby. Babyyyyyy." I watched the episode every single time I went to

Pop Pop's house. I loved my family but I wanted to be a Huxtable so bad.

When the second-oldest Huxtable kid, Denise, was heading to college, she chose Hillman University, a fictitious Historically Black College. This led to a spin-off, *A Different World*, in 1987, which I of course watched religiously every Thursday. The show was my first real glimpse into what education after high school could look like for me. It was the first time I saw Black people being free and expressing culture and joy at an institution of higher education. Even when I didn't understand the jokes, nuances, and plotlines, I felt connected to the show. These were my people and I wanted to be where they were. I knew the show wasn't real, but for thirty minutes I imagined taking a dance class with Kim before grabbing fries at The Pit with Dwayne, Ron, and Freddie, then heading up to my room where Whitley would tell some ridiculous story about a shopping spree with her daddy's money. We'd all laugh and then head to the library to study. It was the life I wanted, the life I craved—but it was only on television.

By the time I got to my senior year and started to look at plans for after high school, college wasn't one of them. *A Different World* had gone off the air in 1993. My senior year was 1994–95, and although I had so many strong memories tied to the show, I knew I didn't have the grades or finances to go to a school like Hillman—or any other college. When the time came for me to apply to schools, I was hesitant but urged by my high school counselors to pick a few places that interested me. That list was short: Hillman College.

Obviously, I was being a smart-ass, leaning heavily into the persona that I did things my own way with little regard for decorum, but when I told my friends, one said, "There is a school like Hillman called Howard in Washington, DC." The deadline for applying to Howard was closely looming, and without looking up anything else about the school—tuition, majors, and all those important details one should know about a potential college—I excitedly sent in all the required information for undergraduate admission to Howard. For someone who didn't apply herself in school and didn't consider herself particularly book-smart, somehow I was convinced I would get into Howard simply because I was Black. That's how I figured all HBCUs worked. I had a very romanticized, naive, and smug view of how they operated, due to only learning about them through a fictional television show. There weren't any conversations about HBCUs with my family or friends, and my high school counselors certainly never posed the option for me, either.

As it turns out, being Black and loving Hillman College wasn't good enough. I got rejected—can you believe it?! Howard let me down gently, however, stating that they would let me know if space became available. I never heard from them again.

I was shattered but kept it straight g, chucking up the deuces while saying FU to Howard. As an act of survival, I learned to meet failure with a hard shell, all the while acting like I wasn't affected or upset. Never let them see you sweat or cry, they say. I wasn't new to the concept of rejection, but this hit me in the gut, perhaps because I was starved for Black culture while at Milton Hershey School, perhaps because the fantasy life I dreamed of slipped away. Howard was supposed to be the place where I found my crew, my own version of Denise, Freddie, Dwayne, Ron, Lena, and Whitley. It sounds so silly looking back, I know. The place where I would be confident walking around with my natural hair because everyone understood and was so accustomed to seeing tight curls that they didn't flinch. The denial shook me in the most upside-down way.

My below-average achievements became magnified once I got that Howard notice because it seemed the predictions from others about the route my life would go if I didn't get my attitude together and grades up were coming true. The rebel that I curated was humbled. The voices became louder and started to follow me, saying I wasn't shit and I was never going to be shit. I scrambled to look for other options, including the state schools around Pennsylvania like Millersville, Shippensburg, and Bloomsburg, where a big chunk of Milton Hershey graduates landed. Even though I was from Philadelphia, no city schools were on my list. I wasn't quite ready to go home yet. I was ready for something completely new.

I finally chose the University of Cincinnati because my mom lived there. She moved there after we went to MHS. Cincinnati wasn't terrible, but it wasn't Philly, or anything close. My saving grace was my best friend, Kerri, whom I met while working at the local amusement park, Kings Island, during the summer of 1994. My brother and I would spend the summers with my mom, and when we got old enough to work, we were expected to get jobs. Kings Island was about thirty minutes away from where I lived, but taking the local bus there daily became an escape for me. I'd pop in my TLC or Bone Thugs-N-Harmony CD and take in all the big houses we'd pass in the suburbs on the way. Even though it got hot outside and park guests could be a lot to deal with, my friendship with Kerri made working at Kings Island worth it—oh, and the cute boys we'd occasionally flirt with. Going to the University of Cincinnati guaranteed that I got to be around her all the time, so I figured it wouldn't be too bad being far from the rest of my family and high school friends.

I arrived on campus two weeks before classes and moved into my dorm, Daniels Hall. I had three roommates. I had only ever lived with the girls who went to my small boarding school—one set of sixteen in middle school and several sets of sixteen in high school, since I shuffled student homes then. So this whole complete-stranger situation made me nervous but excited. At MHS, there was a shared past of coming from difficult situations that also bonded us. With these new roommates, it was different. I didn't know them at all.

I continued my interest in arts and music by joining the marching band color guard, which I had been involved in since junior high school. Upon arriving the first day for tryouts (where all you had to really do was show up), I quickly noticed that out of the entire band, I was one of five Black people, and the only one out of the two dozen in color guard. I knew how to adjust in this environment pretty well. I quickly became friends with some of the white freshman girls who did color guard. We bonded over being new to college as well as being fans of music like Dave Matthews Band, Tori Amos, and Bob Marley. White people love them some Bob Marley. In these girls, I found a crew at the University of Cincinnati.

I loved marching band—the football games, the practices, and being part of Tau Beta Sigma, a band sorority I was recruited to right away. The campus was expansive. I was having so much fun performing at football games, and I loved my new independence. A few months shy of eighteen, I was free to do whatever I wanted, with no one to hold me accountable to anything. I claimed psychology as my major and started classes in the fall of 1995.

The reality of this new environment and independent living hit quick. It all came crashing down after I returned from winter break in 1996, a month or so after I turned eighteen. My grades weren't great; I'd stopped doing assignments due to not understanding the material and really not caring enough to. This led to skipping classes. I owed a balance on my tuition, but I was oblivious to how that affected my school life. I thought that if push came to shove, I would politely ask or beg the

★56★

school not to kick me out—and it would work. That's not exactly how academia works, I found out.

I received a notice in the student portal that I had to report to the bursar's office. I immediately went and they told me I was on academic probation. I figured probation was just the warning before termination, but since I also was behind on tuition, they said I needed to leave school in a few weeks. I had exhausted any financial aid money for the year, and the scholarship Milton Hershey provided its graduates for college only applied if you kept up a decent grade point average, so that wasn't an option.

I was devastated, humiliated, and so embarrassed to tell my roommates and bandmates. I packed up my belongings and moved in with my mom in Cincinnati. In my mind, I was a full adult moving back in with her parents, which had a stigma of failure attached to it. Leaving college sucked but I kept one foot in by continuing to be involved in band. Although I stopped officially going to UC, I still was in color guard there for four years. There wasn't much oversight back then on who was and who wasn't an official student for activities. It was all strange and laughable.

I decided to go work at the local mall. I held down three jobs at the same mall called Carew Tower, which was right in the middle of downtown. I worked at a retail store called Things Remembered, a sandwich shop called Au Bon Pain, and the Omni Netherland Plaza hotel that was attached to the mall. I also spent time with AIDS volunteers in Cincinnati, doing advocacy and clerical work for those infected with HIV. Between band and work I had built up quite a community in Cincinnati, a place of comfort, familiarity, and belonging. I decided to stay in the city a bit. Actually, I had nowhere else to go.

As I was applying for apartments, ready to stop living with my mother, I found out that I had bad credit from defaulting on student loans and multiple unpaid credit cards. The three jobs didn't provide me with enough income for a down payment and first month's rent. I got turned away from several locations before a co-worker let me know that I qualified for housing assistance. This was hard to hear. I had graduated high school, gone to college, had multiple jobs, yet needed to resort to applying for public housing. We were on welfare when I was a kid and I'd sworn never to need that type of help again. I'd also lived in public housing before, and although it wasn't that bad, it wasn't a place where I wanted to be. I felt I'd hit a new low, needing that help as an adult. I was so ashamed, but I took myself down to the housing authority on Gilbert Street in downtown Cincinnati and applied for an apartment.

A stack of forms and interviews later, I was given an apartment that was $150 a month. It was a one-bedroom on the second floor of a four-story building with about forty units. It was located directly down the street from the University of Cincinnati in a section of town called Corryville. My neighbors were mainly elderly Black people. I moved in with just my clothes, a twin bed, and kitchen necessities. Over time I was able to purchase living room and bedroom furniture, a television, and an air conditioner. Kerri was only a fifteen-minute drive away, and I could walk to the grocery store and bus stop in less than ten minutes. There were definitely issues like bugs, noise, and things falling apart sometimes, but this was my very first apartment. I felt grown. I was nineteen years old, and you couldn't tell me anything about life! I was a legal adult living on my own in a way I hadn't before. It's a feeling many get with their first real apartment. I was young and felt so accomplished for standing on my own two feet.

I hung out, danced, and worked my way into my twenties, and after two years I defaulted on my rent and was served an eviction notice with a summons to appear in court. Although an eviction was very serious and it saddened me to be in that position, I was too distracted with other things in life to pay the eviction the attention it needed. I had never been evicted before, or had to appear in a courtroom for that matter, but there was a threat of arrest if I didn't show up, so I did. Something in me was convinced that I would be offered a payment plan in court and allowed to stay in my apartment. That is what I hoped for, but I made backup plans to move in with Kerri's family if I couldn't save my apartment. I spent a lot of time over there anyway, especially after Kerri had her son, Taylor, who was at this point nearly four. They weren't rich, but their house had always been a landing spot for family and friends who were in transition periods. They were also on a bus line that went right downtown to the hotel and mall where

I worked. I showed up to court as instructed, where the property lawyers had all the documentation of me not paying rent.

I had a color guard competition the day I was set to be out of my apartment. Kerri helped me get all the important things moved to her house. I let the other tenants know I'd left my door open if they wanted anything out of there. On the way home from the competition in Dayton, Ohio, I went back to my apartment to see if the key still worked and to make sure I had everything I wanted before I couldn't get back in. It was dark and late. I had a pit at the bottom of my stomach as I turned the corner to my building. As the car inched closer and closer, I immediately saw the contents of my apartment piled up on the curb.

I didn't have any emotion and sort of adopted the attitude that it was what it was. I was twenty-three. I was also going through a major breakup. I'd gone to high school with this man, and I thought we were going to get married. It loomed over my head that he was always too good for me, and an eviction didn't help. He attended and graduated from a top prestigious military school while I was picking up my belongings that had been thrown outside on the street. In many ways, I used that relationship as proof that I was a good, worthy person. I would marry him, go on to be a military wife, have kids, and be seen as honorable—all because I was attached to this upstanding and honorable man. I thought his pureness and excellence would wash away the insecurity and trouble in me. I blamed the breakup on my appearance, lack of education, brokenness, and everything else. I told myself *if* I'd been prettier, *if* I'd graduated college, *if* I wasn't all the things that I was, then maybe, just maybe, he would still want to be with me. It felt like every plan I put in place to have a stable life was falling from underneath me. And that's all I really wanted—a stable life of my own. I felt so stupid for believing that someone would or could change my entire life. I would soon learn that the only person who could do that was me.

Living with Kerri was a dream come true. I'd get up at 6:30 a.m. and take the bus to the mall to work. I knew I couldn't live there forever, so I made a call to my dad in Philadelphia and told him it was time for me to come home. After I had lived with Kerri for four months, Dad drove to Cincinnati and picked me up. He rented a larger car than the one he owned and told me that I could only bring what fit.

Six years after arriving in Cincinnati, I said goodbye to a place that'd defined so much of my life and catapulted me into adulthood. The hardest part was having to say goodbye to Kerri. She was the consistent joyful element in my life while I was in Ohio. The bond that we'd formed transcended friendship, and she flooded me with so much love that it spilled over to how I saw myself. Even now, thirty years into our friendship, this remains the case.

Arriving in Philadelphia in 2001 was a shock to the system. I moved to West Philadelphia into my dad's two-bedroom apartment, which was across the street from a high school. I knew Philly well from when I'd go home to visit family and from extended holidays and summers, so I wasn't uncomfortable in that sense, but I hadn't lived with my dad since my parents had split when I was five. This was going to be interesting for both Dad and me. I also knew this was a temporary solution to my financial and housing issues. I immediately set my sights on getting a job, enveloping myself in the activist and hip-hop scene, and figuring out what I was going to do next with my life. My time in Cincinnati felt so far away, although it had just happened. This was my chance for a new life, a rebirth of sorts in a place where I could start fresh.

I took full advantage of Philly being one of the dopest music cities to ever exist. I was thankful to return to the city during a fire era of neo-soul and hip-hop when amazing hometown talent like Jill Scott, Kindred the Family Soul, Jazzy Jeff, and the Roots were flourishing and holding our city down. There was some type of event almost every night, and none cost more than $10. I quickly found a home on the dance floors of nightclubs like Fluid, shutting the place down with a mix of house and hip-hop dancing. The sun would come up, we'd go home and sleep, then go to work and do it all again the following night. I quickly became a part of the scene, starting to write for websites and papers about artists, shows, and events.

I went to a temp agency and got a three-month job at the Pennsylvania Real Estate Investment Trust, which eventually became permanent. The company focused on office and retail properties. I got busy with organizations like ActionAIDS, which led me to get an additional part-time job at the Youth Health Empowerment Project (Y-HEP), a space for kids in the city to get resources on housing, food, education, and harm reduction. I gravitated toward social work. I was a natural at helping others without judgment. I was able to relate to the teens who came through our door in a way that allowed them to trust me. I was hustling trying to get them what they needed. I saw myself in them. So much of my life was parallel, just with different circumstances. This work made me feel a little more at peace with the missteps I'd made, but it was also a way of showcasing that there was a genuine goodness inside me. I had selfish motives, too: It simply made me feel better about myself to do acts of service. It was what I had to offer the world; it's what I was an expert in. Community work was something no one could take from me. It was a security blanket of sorts that helped seal in a giving reputation that followed me wherever I went, and I was good at it. It gave me a sense of belonging and purpose. I developed close relationships with the kids from Y-HEP and patients from ActionAIDS, so naturally this was what felt good to me.

Since freelance writing and Y-HEP both didn't pay much, nor did they come with benefits, I had to keep a day job for stability. After a year of being at my dad's, I moved into a house with a roommate. With my credit still horrible and a fresh eviction on my record from Cincinnati, there was no way I could get an apartment on my own. Thankfully, a woman my age in South Philly was renting out a room in her house for extra income.

I had settled so very nicely into my new life in Philadelphia. For several years, I continued to thrive. I started and ended a few relationships, saved up enough money to move into my own apartment, started to write for more outlets, continued to tear up dance floors in Philly and in New York, started Cover Your Lover, and was facilitating several teen groups with girls who were in the juvenile detention center and experiencing hardships. It was 2004, and I was truly on a high. The feeling of being less-than was secondary, almost non-existent. Still, whenever the topic of education came up in my professional circles or when the opportunity for a promotion at any job arose, I was confronted once again with the fact that I didn't have a higher education. To make matters worse, there was a time when human resources called me to their office to inform me that my wages would be garnished by the IRS until my student loans were paid off. Student loans for a degree I didn't even get! I was highly regarded and respected at my job, and it was embarrassing.

I loved the work I did with youth so much that I pondered how I could do this full-time. Only problem was that I'd have to go back to school. Even the thought of doing that made me nauseous. How could I afford college? Who would even let me in their school? It took me back to high school again. I had the ghosts of my first college attempt haunting me. But unlike that attempt at college seven years before, I was now mature enough to know what I wanted to do and disciplined enough to pay attention. At twenty-seven, I'd finally found my calling and that was social work. It seemed to feel good and fit right instantly, unlike all my answers to the question of what I wanted to do with my life that I got asked when I was younger. I always felt odd about being twelve and identifying what I wanted to do forever. No one tells you then that you'll figure it out once you have more experiences that shape your view and place in the world.

I didn't know where to begin with college applications, again. I knew I needed to go to a school in the state, specifically around Philadelphia where my apartment and my jobs were located. There was no way I was starting over. I couldn't afford to, mentally, physically, emotionally, and most important financially! After searching for the admissions information on local schools, I very quickly ruled out Drexel, Villanova, University of Pennsylvania, and St. Joe's. One was an Ivy League school, and they all had tuition rates that exceeded my yearly salary. I actually had friends who went to UPenn, so I decided to just talk to them, and they looked at me sideways and actually took pity on the fact that I thought I would get accepted. One harmlessly laughed and said, "You know I graduated at the top of my class, and even *I* had trouble getting in."

I wanted to say, *F you*, but she wasn't wrong.

It took some time, but I applied to several schools. One rejection followed another, then another, followed by another. It stung, but I was prepared for this. Although my life was going well, my insecurities were still hovering over everything I did like a gray cloud that would only let the sun peek through once in a while. This, however, was not one of those times. I had decided in high school that I wasn't smart enough for college, and clearly that was proven correct when I was asked to leave after only one semester in Ohio. And now I'm trying to go back at twenty-seven. I knew the answer would be no, but I still had a little bit of hope in me. You must understand that so many amazing things were happening in my life at this time, it overshadowed me feeling like I didn't deserve any of it. These feelings of doubt were normal to me, nothing that I felt I had to fix. Life would go on, and it did.

One of my final rejections was from Temple University, the college that sat in the heart of North Philadelphia. It was ten blocks from where my father grew up and where my grandmother lived. It sat prominently on Broad Street, convenient to downtown via the train. Temple is a college nestled among the people, embedded in the neighborhood. It's a great school with a great reputation that sees a mix of local students and students from all over the state of Pennsylvania. My brother and sister-in-law went there. For the application, I talked up my community work and showcased my local writing work, hoping this would give me an edge. Well, that didn't quite work, but unlike the other schools, Temple gave me a lifeline by suggesting I take a look at the Community College of Philadelphia (CCP), which was located not too far from Temple's campus. They noted that if I went to CCP for two years and earned my associate's degree, I could take advantage of the transfer program and work toward my four-year degree at Temple, possibly tuition-free if my grades qualified.

I appreciated the offer and even entertained it for a bit before deciding that community college seemed a bit below me. I didn't need to go to community college. I hadn't applied there for a reason. It seemed like a step back, an extension of high school for people who couldn't manage a four-year college, which ironically was me. I would be made fun of or, even worse, flunk out of that, too—and then what? It just wasn't something I wanted to do, but really, it was my only option. I was always afraid people would find out that I didn't actually have a college degree if I told them I was going to community college. I just let people assume that I had a bachelor's. I didn't lie about it, but I also didn't bring it up proactively. I avoided conversations in the workplace about higher education, thankful they didn't happen often. I sat on the idea of community college for a year without taking any steps to actually go. I'm a natural procrastinator but this seemed like a huge undertaking that would take years, and the thoughts about how I would afford it gave me anxiety. That plus the perception of going back to college in my late twenties was so overwhelming. It was too much for me to handle. I did nothing but repeat all of these negative obstacles in my head over and over.

One day I was talking to my dad about the community college offer. He hadn't gone to college, and we really didn't have conversations about education at all. I think he was content with me staying out of trouble and having a job. But he knew how much my work with the community meant to me, and in his own flippant but commanding way he told me I needed to "check it out" and see what community college was all about. I had evolved a bit more in that year, and the ignorant, misguided, and misdirected stance I had on community colleges started to dissolve. I finally applied at the age of twenty-nine and was only conditionally accepted. I failed the math exam and had to take—and pass—night classes at a center for alternative students (mainly located in high schools) in order to start my college courses. Once I did that, I was fully accepted.

I hadn't been in school since 1996. This was 2007, and college just hits way different once you are paying for it with your own money and are a full-fledged adult. I felt like I had another chance. The classes at CCP were smaller than my classes had been my first time in college, and I controlled my pace of learning. Since I'd maxed out all my student loans, I initially paid for my classes by taking cash to the bursar's office. I took six credits a semester, the minimum for the payment plan I was on, the only way I could pay. It would take me four years to complete my associate's degree at this rate, but I pressed on. I didn't have the desire to major in psychology again, but I didn't know what major would point me in the best direction for the social work that I was interested in. In my second semester, I spoke with my women's studies professor, Dr. Conway, about my interests and volunteer work. With her guidance, I decided to declare gender studies as my major. I didn't exactly know what I would do with it, but it was truly just a bridge to get me to Temple to complete my bachelor's degree.

I was juggling several jobs, volunteering, and now a part-time student. I was exhausted, but I also loved being so busy. I had the energy for it, and community college was my speed. I had the most amazing professors who made me and the other students feel like we were at a world-class university, because to me, we were.

As I was rounding out my first year at CCP, the nation was consumed with the 2008 presidential election. I always interpreted elections and politics overall as boring and stale. But even if you weren't into the hoopla of politics, it was *impossible* to ignore the significance of this historic election featuring candidates Hillary Clinton and Barack Obama. It was in your face, everywhere! This wasn't the first time a woman or Black person had run for president of the United States, but it was the first time this country would have one as a major party nominee.

I was intrigued, but I had enough going on. The last thing I needed was to get engrossed in an age-old tradition of choosing a leader for this country who didn't actually fulfill any promises. I was cynical about politics, as many of us are.

Yet I just couldn't escape the Obama blitz. He was truly everywhere, and you couldn't ride down the block, turn on the radio, or watch TV without hearing his name or seeing his face. This guy was on fire, and I kinda, maybe liked it.

CHAPTER 4

Movin' On Up

What are you wearing to the tour today? We have to take lots of pictures—it's our last week!" I texted fellow interns Alisha and Chanel as I was feverishly getting dressed in the morning heading into the final days of my White House internship. A pile of work clothes was covering my twin bed, a sign that I was on struggle street trying to figure out what to wear. Today wasn't just any ol' day. It was the day the interns got to attend the holiday tour. It was a day the interns talked about for weeks, particularly the ones like myself who didn't have access to the executive mansion on a daily basis. This wasn't my first time inside the stark white building, as part of my intern duties was to escort the guests of staff through East Wing tours and my supervisor, Patrick, had taken our department interns on a West Wing tour a few weeks prior. Security was pretty strict and we weren't usually allowed to take any photos inside, but they made an exception for holiday tours. I was extra geeked to document the day, not just to flex a little bit but also for memories, as I didn't believe I'd ever be back in the building again. I planned on taking every photo of myself and the house that I could. This was it and I had to look good.

I was also extremely sad. Three unbelievable adventurous months were coming to a close, including my first time flying on Air Force One with the president and First Lady two months into our internship. While amazing and mind-blowing, the occasion was somber as I was part of the advance team that would assist at the memorial for those who'd been killed and wounded in a mass shooting on the Fort Hood military base in Texas. Since I was just an intern, I was surprised when asked to go, but there were multiple advance teams in Asia preparing for President Obama's visit, so the department was low on people to send to Texas. They also had to pull people from different agencies to help. One of the press leads, Katie, asked me to come into her office. Nervous, I went in expecting her to give me a small office project. She and I were cool, so when I walked in and she asked me to shut the door, I got nervous.

"We're going to be sending you on an advance trip today and don't have too many details yet."

What did she mean, they didn't have too many details yet for somewhere I was going *today*?

I sat silent waiting for these details.

"You can head home and pack for a three-day trip and

we'll have Carpet come pick you up around 4:00 p.m."
Carpet was the internal transportation service, run by
the military for White House logistics.

I still sat silent for more details like where was I
going, what would I be doing, what was I supposed to
be packing, did I need a plane ticket, something?!

Yes, I worked for the government, but that was all
the more reason to know where the hell I was going.

"What weather am I dressing for?" I asked.

"It'll be hot there," she said.

That was it, all the details. I ran back and told my
fellow interns, and they were also confused. I did as
told, went home and packed and waited for the email
that Carpet was outside. It never came. Instead our trip
got moved to the next day and we were to bring our
luggage into work and leave from there. I started to get
a hint that we were heading down to Fort Hood due to
the number of military people involved in the logistics.
In the van on the way to Joint Base Andrews, my suspi-
cions were confirmed.

I loaded into a C-17 military aircraft, which had a
small seat with a flimsy seat belt that was bolted to the
inside of the plane. There was also a full semi-truck
chained down in the middle that would carry the president's limo to Texas. We took off and the whole ride I
kept thinking—*That truck better be secure with those locks.*

We landed in Fort Hood to a grieving community,
met up with the rest of the team, and went into planning mode as the memorial service was due to take
place in forty-eight hours. I assisted with press, making

sure there was space on the risers for all outlets as well as helping to keep them distant from families. I was in tears daily—from exhaustion and sadness, as I saw up close the effects of a mass shooting and the devastation it left on this prideful community of service people.

It seemed trivial, but it was important for me to know how I was getting home, as I had no airline ticket. The lead of our trip told me that the team going back to Washington, DC, would be on Air Force One. "Oh cool, but how am I getting home?" I said. We were all tired but also emotional, so he looked at me with a frustrated face and said, "With us on the plane." I said a casual thank-you but was freaking out inside. Just a few months ago, I was budgeting for my city train pass and now I'm about to ride on the president's actual plane.

But where do I sit? What do I eat? I had been up for nearly two days straight but I didn't want to miss a damn thing, so I was strategizing how to stay awake the whole ride home.

We boarded the plane and a colleague who was the liaison for Veteran and Military Affairs showed me my name on a piece of paper depicting where I was to sit. It said in all-caps: MS. DYER and then a blue-and-white logo that read: WELCOME TO AIR FORCE ONE.

It felt wrong to be excited and I wasn't sure how to hold space for grief and the immense privilege of this moment. I sat down in my very plush chair, buckled my seat belt, and watched my colleagues get extremely comfortable by grabbing blankets and taking naps, getting out their laptops to work, eating snacks, brushing their teeth, and everything else. I was too nervous to do that but was starving so I partook in the salad, bread, and brownie dessert that was served, and it was so, so good.

As I was eating, the president and his personal aide walked around the plane chatting with people casually—as if it were a living room. He had loosened his tie a little bit and had a heavy, sunken expression, which was expected after the memorial service. When he got close to me, I wanted to run and hide. *This man is going to look at me like I'm a stowaway.* He had no idea who I was or why I was there. His aide politely stepped in: "Sir, this is one of our interns, Deesha." I didn't know if I should stand, shake his hand, or what. No one else was standing talking to him. This was the moment, my first-ever real conversation with President Obama. Before I even had a chance to say anything, the president said, "Oh, I didn't know interns were on Air Force One." He started smiling to indicate it was a lighthearted comment.

My embarrassing response is one I will never forget: "I can jump out." I CAN JUMP OUT? WHAT IN THE HELL WAS THAT RESPONSE? WHO IN THE HELL SAYS THAT?

The president said, still smiling, "Good to have you on board," before walking away. It was my one chance to make a good impression and I had just suggested that I would jump off the plane in midair. I don't even know where that came from. An automatic response making myself invisible and scarce. I was horrified, but eventually fell asleep thankful my colleagues around me were knocked out and didn't hear the exchange.

Shrilling from embarrassment, I ended up falling asleep after that and woke up about twenty-five minutes before landing in Maryland. Knowing that I'd never be back on the plane especially after my ridiculous comment, I started to stuff things in my purse as souvenirs. I took the menu, napkins, branded toiletries, and movie selection brochure. I figured there were definitely cameras there, but I didn't care. It was worth the risk!

Now, preparing for my White House holiday tour, I wondered: Would I ever do something as monumental as this again? Did I overall leave a good impression? Would I be remembered as a hard worker who did her best? There was also a real fear of how I would adjust to going back home. Going back to a job that I was thankful for, but had seemed to outgrow. I was a different person now with renewed belief in myself and a glimpse into my potential—but what was next? All of these thoughts flooded my head as I turned from side to side in the mirror checking to make sure the pencil skirt wasn't too short, the chunky sweater wasn't too bulky, the dress flats weren't too old-fashioned, and the hole in my tights wasn't showing. Thank goodness it was my last time having to dress like this. I hated tights. While they weren't a requirement at the White House, I heard my grandmothers' voices in my head anytime I wore skirts or dresses: "COVER THEM LEGS!"

While the reflective questions kept coming up, there was no time for them. I could only think about the exciting tour. I was a guest of the White House today—an actual guest! But first, work, work, work, work, work.

There was nothing unusual about my morning commute that day, except I was filled with anticipation of what the holiday decorations were going to look like. I'd never paid attention to Christmas at the White House before, but it was the first Obama holiday season and the staff chatted a lot about the appointee party where they got to be guests—eating and drinking away. Interns weren't invited to that, but I was still excited to see it all unfold. The social office led by the first Black social secretary, Desirée Rogers, the residence staff, and a host of volunteers chosen from around the country transformed the house into a winter wonderland spectacle, in the most whimsical kind of way. It took over four months to plan, but the execution takes five days, with everything perfectly placed, including the official White House Christmas tree, which is so big that it sometimes has to be trimmed at the top to avoid scraping the ceiling.

My time slot for the tour was 3:00 p.m. I bundled myself in my winter coat and walked around outside from my office in the EEOB to the White House visitor entrance, where I met my fellow interns, Chanel and Alisha, to start the tour. It was everything I'd imagined it to be. Christmas tree upon Christmas tree, sparkling lights, sprinkles of "snow" placed along shiny present boxes and children's toys, the traditional White House crèche placed carefully in the upstairs East Room wall cutout, and enough velvet and glitter bows to wrap the entire building. I took photos in every single room. Ones with just me and ones with me and my friends. We moved slowly, giggling and gawking, until a security officer told us very nicely that we had to move along because there was another tour following us at 4:00 p.m. In addition to the tours, there were nightly parties of up to seven hundred people, which the social office was also in charge of. I couldn't imagine how tired they must be and how they would manage to pull it all off. It all seemed overwhelming. *I don't know how they do it, but it couldn't be me.*

The reality that I'd now have to leave the White House for good hit me after that day as the interns started to wrap up our paperwork, assignments, and duties for the quarter. We received instructions on turning in our badges and computers. My emotions were all over the place, from melancholy to anxious to excited that I was going home to Philly. My living situation had gotten bad as the couple I was rooming with argued more and more. I couldn't wait to get back to my own house. But I was going back a changed person—and the scariest part was that I didn't know what to do with that. Some interns networked their way into positions immediately following the internship, but they were all college graduates already. I didn't think to even express my interest in staying because I didn't have my degree, nor was I even close. Plus, I had no desire to return to the White House; I couldn't even conceive of it. Not because

I didn't like it, but because I felt I wasn't ready. My big break was being an intern and I'd gone as far as I could go with what I had.

I went back to Philly and quickly resumed my life as a part-time student with multiple jobs. I saw nothing wrong with this; most of the other interns were doing the same. What I experienced was a fleeting moment having been chosen to be among the 130 who found themselves at 1600 Pennsylvania that fall. Going back felt different. I felt there was more for me to accomplish out in the world. It was easier to adapt back into a life that was familiar than daydream about a life that didn't exist. It was safer to stay in a box I knew instead of constructing one with an unknown outcome from scratch. The risk was too great to try to build off the White House internship. At the end of the day, I didn't possess a college degree—something acceptable for interns, I thought, but not for staffers. I also wasn't sure how to network using my internship, and I needed to get back to work and make money.

I didn't expect all the excitement from my friends and family when I returned. They couldn't wait to hear all my stories. Whether people were fans of President Obama or not, I came to find out that for them, even knowing someone who worked at the White House was fascinating. Unless you grew up or lived around the DC, Maryland, or Virginia areas or had family who worked in federal service, the chance of you knowing someone who worked in the White House or for a president was pretty slim. It was mysterious, and with this being the first Black president, folks were chomping at the bit to find out any scoop. My co-workers, family, clients, hip-hop crew, friends, and more asked me multiple questions, which I never minded. Even the occasional backhanded compliments from the cheap seats didn't bother me. The "I can't believe they chose you" types that said it with a twang of sarcastic disbelief. But usually, the inquiries were innocent and fell into one of three general buckets.

What was it like working there?

Is he as nice as he seems?

Do you have their phone number?

"It's a whole 'nother world and absolutely crazy but I had the best time" was all I felt comfortable saying. We were given strict orders from the orientation until the end to not talk too much about the details of our internship, to anyone.

"Yes, he is very nice and down-to-earth." I didn't have the heart to tell anyone about the only interaction I had with him on the plane.

The fact that anyone would think an intern might have the Obamas' phone number made me realize that no one really understood how the White House works.

I also had the occasional person ask if I could get a signed letter or photo from their "homeboy" Barack. It was so weird to hear people call him that and to call the First Lady Michelle. Clearly that's their names, but it sounded so informal. Still, it spoke to the masterful way their image created a familiarity with the public. People felt like they knew them in intimate ways that weren't typical of public and government officials, especially a president.

I came back to Philadelphia as a pseudo-celebrity, the person who was one degree from the Obamas. As I settled back into the hustle that was my life before I'd paused it to do the internship, I couldn't shake how much I had accomplished in the last few months. I was searching for that part of me that was able to quiet the fear enough to go for such a big opportunity. My head felt higher than the clouds, in a humbling way that allowed me to see things that had escaped me before, like how far I could go if I stretched myself and bulldozed past all that scared me. What else could I do, what else could I actually become? I was curious.

I wrestled with these questions. I'd go to work at the real estate firm thinking about how I had walked in the White House every single day with my face on a light-blue badge that read INTERN. As the time got further from that December day I'd left, it became less about the building, the access, or even the president and First Lady. Thinking about those months nudged me toward what I thought was the impossible, things that were beyond all I could imagine. Picturing my badge reminded me that I could do hard things. That nudge became mentally painful after three months back at my regular job and life. I started to brainstorm the various ways I could explore how far this high could take me.

I didn't exactly need to be in politics or the White House. I didn't know where I would go or what I wanted to do; I just knew I couldn't stay where I was. That was the one thing I was sure of. But how was I going to do it exactly? First, I needed to leave my real estate job, but it provided me with income and insurance—plus, they had just supported me financially as I left for three whole months. How could I turn around and leave? My other jobs were all part-time, and none came with benefits. The nudge kept interrupting these thoughts, making sure I remembered it was there.

This nudge was confirmed by a trip that I took with the White House advance team on behalf of President Obama to St. Louis, Missouri, in March 2009, three months after my internship ended. Advance volunteers are people who get paid a day-rate to travel on behalf of the White House when the president or First Lady has an out-of-town event. These advance volunteers are usually former interns, people from campaigns, or those who know someone in the Scheduling and Advance Office. These roles are not filled by White House employees, and you only get paid when you go on a trip. The trips were usually five to seven days, and there was no guarantee that you would be continuously called to do one. It was unstable but I was familiar with the roles and responsibilities of advance work from my internship, making my learning curve a little less steep. My name was on the list of people to call since I was just recently an intern.

It was pretty bold of me to walk into Jon's office and tell him I needed to take vacation days after three months of being gone. He somehow agreed to this, most likely realizing that it was a big deal for me to stay connected to the White House. I helped out with the press on that trip. Everything from setting up press risers, helping satellite trucks park early in the morning, checking press in, and handing out badges, to making sure everyone had an accessible spot to film, take photos, or record the remarks. I had never been to St. Louis before and it was a small taste of what life on the road full-time could be like, going from city to city on behalf of the White House. The days were long and the work was hard, but I felt useful and challenged. My adrenaline rushed every day going to trip meetings or calls. It felt powerful to be a representative of the White House, even on a temporary basis—as I had to remind myself that it wasn't a full-time role.

After the trip, I went home and decided that going without a salary, benefits, 401k, and everything else that comes with stable employment was worth it. It was a position I had been in before. And just like then, I'd figure it out. But what about the money? I had bills to pay and I didn't want to get in a situation again where I defaulted on them. I checked my bank account to see how many months I could actually last without steady income. Thanks to the money that was gifted to me from my co-workers and CEO before I left for Washington, plus the fact that I was extremely cost-conscious while living in DC, my bank account showed over $7,000. This was also before the taxman cometh for half. It was the most money I'd ever had in the bank, and it would cover over six months of bills. By then, I would hope to have another steady job somewhere else.

I decided to throw caution to the wind and email my intern supervisor. I told him I wanted to continue to do advance work for President Obama as many times as possible. There were so many trips—at least ten a month. Each team was staffed with seven to nine people. The absence of a day job gave me availability to go on whatever trip I was called to do. I would make myself available for anything at any time to go anywhere. If I did four trips a month, that'd be enough to pay some bills while I figured out the next step. Advance couldn't be forever, but it served as a holding pattern.

Messy and scared, I gave my notice at my day job in April. I didn't quite have the right words to articulate or communicate why I was leaving. I felt disheveled and unsure more than once after I gave the resignation. It was all foreign to me, and it was hard. Many of my co-workers had become my friends, as evidenced by their financial support of the internship. It was far from what I really wanted to do, but there was safety and security there. It afforded me my own place, a decent salary, and flexibility to pursue other things like school and volunteering. I had a fear that I'd never get a job like this again, especially without higher education, but I now knew what I *could* do, so I took the chance.

The first week of May would be my last time walking into the job I'd held for nine years. When Monday of that week came, I thought about taking back my resignation. I went through a moment of feeling foolish for leaving my good job for something as unpredictable as advance. I also decided to leave my other jobs, except freelance journalism. Believing in myself enough to make this move without my imposter syndrome interfering to tell me that I didn't deserve to try was a rare occurrence. I had to trust in the universe, God, and most important myself.

My last week was full of goodbyes, happy hours, packing up my cubicle, and shuffling my work to another assistant who would take over my responsibilities until they hired someone else permanently. It was spent emailing contacts—everyone from facility vendors to New York bankers—to let them know I was leaving to go to advance for President Obama. No one understood what that was, but they all seemed happy for me. Although I planned to do advance, there was no guarantee that I would be slated (the term used for being placed on a trip). I stretched the truth justifying my departure just a little, but I wanted to appear as if I already had something better than where I was. I wanted to seem more valuable. It fed my ego to have people think I was quitting to go to the White House. I never lied, just sort of danced around it and let people come to their own conclusion. I felt important.

With only two days left until I walked out of my Center City Philly office for good, I received an email from Alyssa Mastromonaco. During the internship, Alyssa was like a mythical figure to us. As the head of the Office of Scheduling and Advance, she sat in the West Wing. She and her assistant were the only ones who worked out of there, while the rest of the department was in the adjacent office building. I was standing up at my desk sealing up boxes when the message popped up. My eyes widened and I may have actually stopped breathing for a few moments.

I was afraid to open it and a mountain of questions went through my head. *What can she actually want? What did I mess up that they are just finding out about? Did I forget to pay my cafeteria bill before I left? No, it can't be that. She has more important stuff to do.* I pulled out my fancy office chair and nervously sat down to read.

> *Deesha, I understand you may be in town this week (or early next). I would love a few minutes to sit down and chat. We have an opening in our department here at the White House that I would like to discuss. If you have any interest in being considered for this position I would like to talk or meet as soon as possible. Hope you are well, Alyssa*

Holy shit. What? What? WHAT? I was shocked and confused. Didn't Alyssa know I didn't have a college degree? Hadn't she heard about the dumb comment I made to the president on Air Force One? I know she reviewed the résumés of incoming department interns, so clearly she had to know I was still in school. Anxiety then set in as I thought about how I would tell her thank you, but no thank you—as it'd be less embarrassing than letting her know about my education status. I was used to letting myself down before others had a chance to. It was a comfortable place for me. The imposter syndrome was back. I started a Word document and drafted different ways to respond.

> *Dear Alyssa,*
> *It is great to hear from you. Thank you for your offer. Working at the White House would be a dream, but I am still in school and need to turn this down.*

No, that's weird to say it would be a dream. Rework.

> *Dear Alyssa,*
> *How are you? It is great to hear from you. I had the best time being an intern but am still in my first year of community college and—*

Ugh. What comes after that?

> *Hi Alyssa,*
> *Great to hear from you. I'm unsure if the team told you, but I'm still in college. Maybe the position will be open in 2 years? Haha!*

Well, that's dumb. Haha? This is a senior official at the White House. Who says haha?

Alyssa was actually closer to me in age than any of the Scheduling and Advance staff so I always felt that *we've lived life and experienced real shit* bond with her. Like we'd be friends if I wasn't an intern, but I was and she wasn't. I'd been working on this response for a good twenty minutes as my co-workers kept coming by my desk to give me goodbye hugs. I didn't want to appear too eager in my response or response time, so I got up and walked to the bathroom. As I washed my hands, I looked in the mirror and whispered to myself, "This is mad. What? I just got an email from the White House about a job." I didn't want to tell anyone about the email until I responded. I didn't want their follow-up questions about the salary, position, duties, and whether I'd be in close contact with the president if I took the job. Although I knew the answers, I didn't want others getting hyped on my behalf, inflating and twisting my reality that this could actually happen. I also wanted to enjoy the moment. The email from Alyssa was only several lines, but receiving it felt like a victory in a way. A victory over all the obstacles from my childhood to my adulthood that put me in a space to question who the fuck I was. This simple email.

It was 5:30 p.m. Thirty minutes had passed and I had to respond. I sat back down in my wheelie chair, swiveling it from left to right, left to right on the plastic mat underneath. *Okay, here goes.*

> *Good Afternoon Alyssa,*
> *Thank you so much for sending this email and wanting to speak with me about the position. I am definitely interested in speaking with you. I will be available from Tuesday– Friday of next week. Wednesday is the*

craziest day out of all of them, but I'll make it
work according to your schedule.
Looking forward to hearing from you,
Deesha

Sent, 5:36 p.m. She replied five minutes later, adding her assistant into the email to set up a call for the very next day. I wasn't nervous, I was baffled and still in disbelief. I couldn't really focus on anything after that and headed home, where I shared the news with a few friends via text, who reacted exactly like I knew they would—brimming with excitement, followed up by numerous phone calls with loads of questions about the job, the call, moving to DC, literally everything. I appreciated their enthusiasm but told them to calm down because they were making me nervous by filling my head with all these hypothetical scenarios.

I didn't know how to prepare for the call. The role was the associate director of scheduling correspondence. I would be in charge of processing, managing, and responding to scheduling requests from the public for President Obama and also overseeing the internship process for the department. I would be the one making the phone calls late at night to interview potential hopefuls for a White House internship. This made me the most excited, to be able to change someone's life as mine had been from Patrick's phone call nearly a year ago.

This was just a phone call to gauge my interest in

the role, not a job interview, Alyssa's assistant told me, but I knew I had to treat it like one and be prepared. But I had no idea what questions she would even ask that I could practice. Maybe my experience being an intern and questions around how I enjoyed the responsibilities? If she asked me about managing interns, I would pivot into the mentoring work I'd done with younger people. While it was not the same, I could make that answer work.

I winced at how to tell her I was still in college. I wanted to make this known up front to avoid it coming out after a job offer or starting the role. If that was going to be a roadblock, I wanted to address it as soon as possible. Perhaps I should have added that in the response to Alyssa's email, but I felt it best to have an actual conversation about it. My life experience was surely equivalent to a master's degree, but this is the White House we're talking about here. They want institutional degrees, and I understood that.

I didn't sleep too well that night, tossing and turning thinking about how the conversation would go. She was calling in the morning at 10:00 a.m., after her daily briefings. It was my second-to-last day at work, so I took a half day off to be home for the call. Thankfully this was before the days of video calls and I didn't need to get fully dressed with hair and makeup. It gave me time to sleep in and grab my favorite—a cinnamon raisin bagel with cream cheese and jelly—from the bodega around the corner during my morning walk with the dog. I kept checking my phone to make sure it was charged and that I didn't miss any calls from any unknown numbers. We had a set time, but I was ready early. Alyssa was busy and could dial me at any time if her schedule changed. Ten minutes before the call, I grabbed some paper, a pen, and my laptop, ready to take notes or look up information while on the phone. I wanted to be ready.

My dining room table was located by a window to the alleyway on the side of the house that could get pretty noisy, so I made a makeshift desk out of two TV trays in the living room in front of the couch. The dog was in the next room, chewing on a bone I gave him to keep him distracted. I sat down and waited for the call. At exactly 10:00 a.m., Alyssa's assistant emailed me.

> Hi Deesha,
>   Running a little late. She'll call shortly.
> Sorry for the late notice.

Five minutes later, she called. She apologized for running a little late and said she was excited to talk to me. I politely said the same. She wasted no time getting right to the point—there was an opening in the department and when she asked employees who they thought could fill the role, multiple people mentioned my name. She went on by telling me that the job was mine if I wanted it, and it started in three weeks, by June 1, because that was when the summer interns started. She told me to quickly send my résumé to the chief of staff's office and pending the security check and drug test (both of which

I had no worries about), she'd be delighted to welcome me to the department. She ended with, "Do you have any questions?" *Excuse me?! Yes, I have lots of questions!*

We'd only been on the phone five minutes and everything was spinning in my head. I knew that she was pressed for time, so I needed to be quick with these questions. I didn't want to annoy her. I had to say something about school. I was less concerned now about how I would be perceived than her thinking I was wasting her time on this damn phone. "I'm still an undergrad at community college. I went back to school at an older-than-normal age, so I don't have a degree." It was out there—for better, for worse—a weight had been lifted. There wasn't time to think about the gravity of that moment. I asked her if it was okay that I was still in school, and that I would like to try to continue going online if I took the job.

"Yes, of course. It can be figured out. Do you have any other questions or want time to think about it? We need to move quickly," she said. No kidding—June 1 was only three weeks away and I had to figure out moving to Washington, DC, and starting a new job AT THE WHITE HOUSE. What if they found someone else in the time that I was thinking it over?

"I'm interested and I accept the job. Thank you so much."

"Great. We're excited." The call was ten minutes long. In just ten minutes, my life had completely flipped again.

I hung up the phone and let out a big scream, a shout of emotions that had been building up since I'd received the email yesterday. I started to cry, staring at my phone wondering who I should tell first. My dog rushed in the room after hearing my noises, and I motioned for him to sit on the couch and said, "Change, I'm going to the White House." He looked at me expressionless, like—*That's nice, lady, do I get a treat for this?* I took the job without consulting anyone. This was my decision and my life. I felt such power and excitement, fear and panic. I had to tell everyone, find a place to live, and leave my world, my city, my close-knit community. I made the decision with disregard to my relationship, which I felt bad about but I figured we could work out the distance. Philadelphia and DC weren't that far apart, really?

I called my brother, my parents, and Kerri. They were so excited but had more questions than I had answers. It was all happening so fast. It was truly unbelievable. I'd always felt like such a flawed human being overshadowed by insecurity and hard experiences that derailed my potential. *How, how is this happening to me?*

I had an hour to get to work. Still in complete disbelief, I rushed to get ready and sprinted toward the 34 trolley to head downtown. I couldn't wait to tell my boss, but was hesitant to mention it to the rest of my co-workers just yet. I wanted a day for it to soak in and better figure out how to explain to everyone what exactly I'd be doing in the job. Explaining scheduling and advance work to people not in politics is sometimes a challenge. Jon was so happy for me. He was already prepared for me to leave at the end of the week, so it wasn't like this meant he was losing me to the White House. He asked when he could tell the other executives. "Not yet," I said.

I was already mentally checked out from the job so I spent all day researching apartments. I still didn't have the best credit, and with the eviction, I was scared to try for my own place. I instead looked for roommate situations, this time staying away from divorces. I wanted to live with women, hopefully ones in their thirties and above like me. I kept the price range between $400 and $500 a month, and I needed to be near a train line and get to work AT THE WHITE HOUSE within thirty minutes. I also didn't know DC at all—I pretty much went to the same four places when I was an intern (Busboys and Poets; the supermarket and the train station near my deep Southeast room share; and Union Station to catch the bus and train back to Philly). I made a few appointments to see places on my trip down to DC the following week. I'd already heard from the White House that my drug test needed to be done in person. I also had to take care of the other details that come with starting a federal government job. On this trip, I hoped to find a place and schedule a move-in date.

The next day was my last day of work and I wasn't focused at all. I was anxious to get out of there so I could go home and pack. All of my emotion was caught up in this pending new life. The days between my last job and my DC housing trip were minimal. The rush of it all didn't allow me time to digest, breathe, and take in all that was happening.

Before getting the bus in Philadelphia for my DC visit, I snagged a Philly soft pretzel and iced tea at the Gallery Mall, which was across from the dodgy Greyhound bus station, and stood in line for the bus. I had money for an Amtrak train, but wanted to save as much as I could until my first paycheck from the White House. I hadn't bothered to ask how much I was getting paid and when. I'd planned on leaving my position without a steady job anyway. I added "ask about salary" to my to-do list.

The whole ride down on I-95, I slept. All the flurry of activity had caught up to me. When I woke up, we were in DC and I had to rush off to my first apartment appointment in Southeast DC. A woman with black curly hair and a huge smile answered the door and welcomed me in. The house was on the corner of a transitional neighborhood that had a fire station down one street and a shelter way down the other street. I immediately loved the vibe, as it was far enough from government buildings to feel local, but also close enough to remember that we were in DC. It mixed the local and transient crowds well. The house was beautiful, with a nice backyard, huge kitchen, cozy living room, and three bedrooms, the smallest of which would be mine. We'd all share a bathroom as well as the common spaces. Besides the owner, there was another professional woman living there. She also was very nice, and we all three talked a bit after the tour. I felt comfortable there, like I'd be friends with these ladies outside the housing situation. I'd found my place.

I met with some former co-workers for coffee. I was so happy to see them again, and we plotted about hanging out once I came on board full-time. They had to run back to work, but I stayed for a bit in the coffee shop to soak up my new permanent city.

The next day Alyssa and I had a brief call where I asked about my salary. To my surprise it was lower than what I was making at the real estate job. I was completely shocked that White House employees didn't make more, but that wouldn't stop me.

Within two weeks, I packed up my whole life. I had no idea when I'd be back in my beloved city. Would it be 2012 after the presidency was up? Would I find my place in politics and stay in DC? I had no intention of leaving the White House until it was time. This was a chance to live and build history. I was staying put as long as I could.

One the eve of my first day, I got out my computer and typed this email:

> *Hey everyone—*
> *I hope this email finds you well. As of*
> *the first week of June, I will be leaving Philly*

and moving to DC to become the Associate Director of Scheduling Correspondence for the White House. After my internship, I moved back home, went back to my job and school. Well, there was an opening in my old department and I am so blessed to have it offered to me.

I want to thank you for the years of support you have shown me while doing my thing in Philly. I do believe that taking this job will allow me to do just as much for the community as I did at home. DC has a huge AIDS population as some of you may or may not know and I look forward to volunteering down there.

I've found a place and will be moving early June (yikes!!). I never thought I'd be working at the White House...seriously, but it just goes to show you what is possible if you stay focused and invest in yourself and your community a bit. I always knew that I could, but I never thought that I would. When I interviewed for the internship last fall they asked me how I will use the internship to change things. I told them that just me going is showing young women... especially of color that they could do anything. I hope this move and opportunity continues to do just that. If you guys visit DC, let me know.

Thank you for all the prayers, heartaches, and love…each part got me to where I am today.

I sent it as a blind copy to a few people, namely two ex-boyfriends, a high school principal, and a few frenemies.

I knew it was petty and I didn't care. I wanted them to see and feel how they'd discarded, disrespected, mishandled, and mistreated me—and I still rose. If I could have called them all and cussed them out, I would have for making me feel as if I wasn't good enough, as if I didn't matter, as if I would never do anything worthy in my life.

I had actually done plenty worthy by this point, but working at the White House for President Obama couldn't be argued with. I received a response from only two people. They hit me with the "Wow, Congratulations," to which I never responded. The victory that day, that moment—was mine.

On June 1, 2010, I entered the White House as a full-time employee. I walked in the building that morning with bright eyes, heavy nerves, and all of the optimism that one could possibly muster walking in as an employee of the first Black president and First Lady. I felt so good, as if I'd put to bed all my disbelief about what I could and couldn't do. I took a deep breath walking into my old office to take a seat at Patrick's former desk. I hugged all my former co-workers.

It was 9:30 a.m. and I still didn't have a work

computer or phone, and in an hour, the six department interns that I was in charge of would arrive. It wasn't ideal that we all would start on the same day, but as I would come to find out, the White House is organized, unpredictable chaos all the time. I picked up the summer interns in the South Court Auditorium, remembering being in that position just nine months prior. I took the winding stairs down one floor to the auditorium where all the intern supervisors were gathering. Some were startled to see me. "I just got hired! It's my first day." It felt good to say I'd just gotten hired.

The intern coordinator called off each department, until it got to ours. Before I could even blink, there were seven (ooof, I'd thought it was six!) interns right in my face smiling these big smiles. We walked down to the employee cafeteria called Ike's and sat down at the tables and chairs for informal introductions. One by one, they told me who they were and where they went to school. From Georgetown to Duke to Ball State, all of them were attending or had graduated from amazing four-year colleges, and here they had a boss who'd failed out of and then couldn't even get into one, her only option being community college. Somehow I was supposed to guide them through this experience when my only qualifying factor seemed to be that I'd already done it and they hadn't. But was that enough?

As each intern explained their educational and professional accomplishments, I started to feel like maybe I wasn't the right person for this job and Alyssa had just needed someone quick to manage them—it wasn't that she thought I was qualified. This woke my imposter syndrome up. I thought it was gone. I thought getting this job put it to rest for good.

There is never a good time for self-doubt to show up, never, but this shit always flared at the busiest time, when I had no energy or space to combat the many self-loathing thoughts that were entertaining my mind.

I don't have time for this.

I don't have time for this.

I DON'T HAVE FUCKIN' TIME FOR THIS.

"Oh, you'll get to know all about me throughout the summer," I told the interns. "Let's show you around and go meet the team." I dodged that bullet of having to tell them I was a freshman who happened to be an intern last year. I made up scenarios of how they would respond. Would they still respect me as their boss if they knew I wasn't as educated as them? I told myself: *Probably not.*

But they wouldn't find out today, and probably not for a while.

CHAPTER 5

Ascending: Becoming the White House Social Secretary

I came in the door, I said it before. I never let the
mic magnetize me no more.
—Eric B. & Rakim

Every morning I picked a different song to listen to from the train stop that let me off ten minutes from the White House. It ranged in genre depending on my mood or what kind of workday I was walking into. On this particular morning, I was feeling like I needed a little boost, and hip-hop could always do that for me. I pulled up my playlist of favorites like Missy Elliott, A Tribe Called Quest, the Roots, Rakim, and Nas. I was almost a year into being a full-time employee at the

White House and in the midst of having my third intern class. My feet were more planted and secure in the job. I had a routine down of mentoring the interns and getting requests to meet with the president pushed up the command chain. I had gotten a loose handle on the reality that I was no longer an intern, but now a staffer with an official green badge that gave me access to the complex, except the West Wing. Those with that access had navy-blue badges. They were fancy.

In addition to the intern and correspondence responsibilities, I was able to do a few advance trips, including one to Jakarta, Indonesia, with President Obama. It was my first international trip, my first time in Asia, and my first time flying business class (!!!!), which we got to do if the destination was over twelve hours away. President Obama was partially raised in Indonesia, so it was special to be on this trip and witness how adored he was by the country and its people. I assisted at the main event site, which was a speech at the University of Indonesia. I was there for a total of fifteen days, while the president was in the country for four days. Despite the very hot weather, travel delays, and challenges like spotty electricity for a large-scale event, I absolutely loved everything about being behind the scenes to make this homecoming for the president happen.

On this trip, I also got exposed to embassies and consulates, which work closely with the White House and State Department on diplomatic visits. I had never stepped foot inside a US embassy before and this one was beautiful, a nondescript building on the outside but the inside was full of art, flowers, and modern interior design. I felt so official walking in the security gate to have my diplomatic passport scanned. When I said to the armored guard, "I'm with the White House," he'd immediately let me through for our daily meetings. The embassy served as our eyes and ears on the ground, a pivotal bridge between the foreign and American governments, but also working out any challenges over language, access, housing, and more. This trip confirmed that I wanted to be on the road more than I wanted to be in the office. But I was also just thankful to be there, so exploring an advance role as a full-time employee seemed a bit, well, *ambitious*? Being at the White House was already a reach, and the only advance roles that were opening up in our department were trip leads—and I definitely wasn't ready to be in charge of an entire trip.

I feel the wind, five, six, seven, eight, nine, ten (nine, ten), Missy "Misdemeanor" Elliot sang as I removed my headphones, threw my belongings on my desk, and ran over to the microwave to make tea before heading to the cafeteria to buy a bagel. The interns were out today helping with an in-town event for the president. As they were nearing the end of the semester, I tried to get them out of the office as much as possible to experience the advance side of our department. It was also wonderful to have time to myself. The department had shifted office spaces a bit, leaving me to share my large office space with three interns. There was never privacy. I was taking this day to prepare for the new incoming interns in four weeks and imagine what it would be like to have this huge office by myself with windows that looked over 17th Street. It was heavenly.

While enjoying the silence and typing away, my BlackBerry, which was sitting on my long dark wood desk, started to ring. This was odd because I hadn't given the number out to anyone but those in the White House, and we never actually called one another. Everything was done by email—everything. I also didn't get many scam calls.

"Hello, this is Deesha."

"Hey, Deesh."

The voice on the other end was my friend Greg who was a scheduler in our department. We'd clicked immediately when I was an intern. Greg is Black; he's from New Jersey and just had a little girl with his wife. He was younger, but would always look out for me. He was one of the many who gave my name to Alyssa for the job.

"You got a second?" he said.

"Sure, what's up? Where are you anyway?"

He was on his way to the office but wanted to alert me that the hotel director in our department was going to be leaving. She hadn't officially announced it yet but some folks knew. Greg knew of my desire to travel more, so he wanted to give me the heads-up.

"I would have no idea how to do that job," I laughed.

"You should talk to Danielle about it soon if you are interested."

Danielle was the director of scheduling and one

of the five Black women that I worked with. She was from the Pacific Northwest, but she'd gone to an HBCU in Virginia, so I claimed her as an East Coast girl. She worked down the hall from Senator Obama's office in the Senate, and went to his team upon the announcement that he was running for president. She was part of the core group that stood beside him on election night. She was also younger than me.

I knew if I asked her about the job, she wouldn't laugh in my face like I had lost my mind, being on this job less than a year and already asking to move up to another role. I worked with Danielle a bit as an intern and we talked openly about random stuff all the time. She was another one who put my name forward for the job and said, "I knew you'd be good when you put 'Closer' by Goapele as your favorite song on the internship application." Well, I do love that song, and the lyrics are so perfect:

Sometimes you just have to let it go, leaving all my fears to burn

I emailed her that I wanted to have a quick chat, to signal that it was nothing *too* serious. She immediately wrote that I could stop by her office in the next hour. Her office was only three doors down from mine and she had privacy with doors that shut—unlike some offices that didn't have doors from room to room.

"What's going on? You aren't leaving, too, are you?" she asked with a worried smirk. I asked her about the hotel director position and if it was really going to be open soon. She quickly shot back, "Yep, you interested?" The conversation was quick and easy. If I didn't get it, I was completely fine, and if I did, I'd be ecstatic. I was content with my role, but being able to travel for work and see the world would be a bonus.

A few hours later, the person vacating the position came to my office to confirm that she was leaving and the job would be vacant. At this moment, I started to think that this might really happen. I *could* take on another role. She explained the responsibilities—booking hotels, handling everything from keys to the motorcade at the hotel, and working with multiple departments. She wanted to prepare me for an interview about the position. In this role, I would also have brief interactions with the president and First Lady while they were at the hotel. I had zero interaction with them in my current role. Of course, the Philly girl who took to the streets dancing in the rain after his election would have been beside herself for the president to know her name and face, but I truly didn't want that. I liked being a worker bee, behind the scenes as much as possible.

The process for filling this new role moved quickly because there was a ton of travel coming up and there was no way the role of hotel director could be vacant. To my utter surprise and after talking with other leadership, I was given the job a week after my initial conversations with Greg and Danielle. I was too busy in the transition to think about whether I was qualified or not, so those natural feelings of doubt stayed at bay. If anything, this was actually a job I did have some experience in. One of my many jobs before the White House was as a receptionist at a hotel, so I did have a knack for hospitality.

Being in the same department with the people also made it fun. The majority of them were easygoing and not as snooty as I would expect White House employees to be.

This would probably be the closest I would come to fulfilling my dream of being a TV host, traipsing around gorgeous hotels on someone else's dime. In this case, taxpayers'—so basically I *was* paying for these trips myself. I loved everything from negotiating contracts with global hotel brands, to staying in four- and five-star hotels that I definitely couldn't afford on my own, to showing up to meetings with top hotel leaders wearing my huge gold hoops. I heard more than once, "Are you the person in charge of the VIP accommodations here?" from suit-wearing general managers and their staff.

"Yes, that's me, now let's get started."

I could always tell they expected someone else. Sometimes they would skip right over me to ask my Secret Service counterpart in the room about overall planning, room assignments, and schedules. This was usually a white male, whom I guess "looked the part." The agent would reiterate that he was security and protection only, and for everything else, he'd defer to staff. That's me.

At the White House, my role was considered a junior position but out in the field and on the road, I felt powerful. I enjoyed the logistics of making a home away from home for the Obamas wherever they went. This afforded me the opportunity to touch down on four continents for the first time: South America, Asia, Africa, and Australia.

But this didn't all come as naturally as I wished. My learning curve was steep. My first solo trip after my training was in Denver, Colorado. The president, his Secret Service detail, and his then-personal-aide Reggie pulled up to the loading dock at the hotel. They were all in the presidential limo, called The Beast, while traveling staff were piled in passenger vans that trailed behind in the motorcade. The weather was cool in Denver, but after running around making sure everything was ready for the boss and over seventy-five staff members, I was sweating profusely. I could feel the edges of my relaxed hair curling up as I stood next to the large trash bins in the dock. I carried my trusty clipboard, which had the schedule, everyone's room numbers, and information about the hotel gym, Wi-Fi, and restaurants clipped to it. I read and reread everything about fifty times before the group arrived. Weighing on my skirt was a heavy walkie-talkie radio with a wire up my back connecting to an earpiece, and a wire down my sleeve connecting to a microphone. These radios allowed me to communicate with the rest of the advance team. One of my skirt pockets was full of multiple hotel keys, and the other pocket held my BlackBerry and mints. Breathing quietly but heavily, I watched as the president stepped out of the limo. This would be my first longer interaction with him since Fort Hood. *Please dear God let him not remember me as the intern who said she'd jump out of a plane.*

"Welcome to Denver, sir."

"Hi there, thank you. How's the hotel?" He would ask this at almost every stop, like we were ever going to say anything that wasn't pleasant.

"It's very nice, you'll enjoy it."

"Well, that's good."

As we started to walk into the back hallway, past the kitchen and to the service elevators being held for us, I panicked about the staff not knowing where to go or how to get there, although everyone had been emailed their room number and arrival directions. I couldn't remember if I had another advance staffer helping them get to the primary floor. For security reasons, guest elevators don't stop on the president's floor while he is staying there, nor do they stop one floor above or below. So we'd arranged for staff to take the other service elevator, which would be operated by security, to the primary floor of the hotel. There I was in the elevator with the president, *freaking out internally about the staff.*

When our elevator hit his floor, the doors opened up. I got out and stood there waiting for the other elevator to come up, so I could help the staff. I assumed someone else knew where the president's room was, so they'd walk him there. Instead the entire crew of folks in my elevator stood there with me for a split second until the president looked at me, confused, and Reggie said, "Deesha, which way do we go?" The hotel floor was massive, and I left the president standing in a hallway trying to figure out which way his room was. I was in charge of the most important detail, with the most important person in the country, and I looked like a total idiot in front of him. This time I was a full-time employee who was expected to know better.

It is quite a chaotic scene when the president arrives—there's his luggage plus all the staff's luggage, the handing out of hotel keys, scheduling people on elevator runs to their secure floors, credit card authorizations, and everything else that comes with over a hundred people arriving at the same time at a hotel with you in charge. That "you" was me and, after it all died down, I went to my room and cried. I for sure thought the president and Reggie would tell Alyssa how awful I was at such a simple task and I'd be fired. In this job and others at the White House, there wasn't a margin for error. Mistakes came with a hefty price tag. The stakes were too high to mess up. The president's security and well-being were in our hands. I beat myself up over this for a long time. I felt so much humiliation.

This embarrassing incident was more than enough to scare me. I got through that travel visit, and so many others, for two years after that. I never made that mistake again, and the president never again had to guess which way he was going! To this day, I'll travel with the former president and First Lady once in a while, and I am still very, very direct about their movements, to the point where, on the last trip to Australia (as I was writing this book), the president said, "Deesha, we got it, don't worry." But of course, Denver still haunts me, and I still worry.

After the election of 2012, when President Obama won another term, I started to get antsy. I had also completed my coursework to graduate from community college, four years after starting, but couldn't attend graduation because I was busy getting a president to serve another four years, which I thought was a pretty great excuse!

As we were rounding into the new year, there were a lot of changes, and many of the co-workers whom I had known since my intern days were moving on to other opportunities, mainly outside of government. I was spending more time on the road than in the office—which is what I wanted, but challenges started to arise. I'd always thought I was someone who essentially got along with most people. A problem with authority sometimes? Sure. I never had to fight too much for respect or decency from others, at least since boarding school. This was about to change when I became known as a fighter, defiant, the *you know she's from Philly* Deesha.

The thing about imposter syndrome is that even when you're managing it well, possibly even fooling yourself into thinking you have overcome it, it creeps right back up when challenging or new situations arise. This is natural and makes complete sense because we aren't supposed to know how to handle everything. We default to what we know, using the tools that have helped us overcome and survive. We are designed to keep learning. Institutions are dedicated to just this, continued learning, and no matter how much people may act like it, no one knows everything.

The shift began when someone questioned my intelligence and qualifications. What may have been a typical exchange for some people was what I'd always feared, exposing me as an imposter. I was caught between two versions of myself—the person who wanted to snitch and fight versus the person who wanted to cave and sink to the criticism. I was stuck either way. I'd be called defensive or a complainer who blew things out of proportion. I balanced between the two versions, walking into work with little patience and closed fists. I did my job but stayed ready for whatever was going to come my way.

I was told point-blank that I had an attitude, and I completely agreed. I had a right to my attitude after the attempt to devalue what I knew I brought to the table. This is not to be confused with how much honor I felt. I loved being there, the movement I was part of, the fun that I had, and the friends I made. But I learned the hard way that having conflicting feelings is normal; they all can exist at the same time in the same place. A restaurant called Busboys and Poets had become a refuge for me. Nestled on bustling 14th Street, about fifteen minutes from the White House, this space was built for poets, activists, thinkers, and creatives who needed a place to land, to write, to breathe. It sits on the edge of Howard University and draws the students to its walls to study and be in community. The walls were painted with quotes and photos from Langston Hughes, Audre

Lorde, and James Baldwin, while the music was always a mix of jazz, Afrobeats, and hip-hop. It had a bookstore that sold the classics but also works from independent authors of color that you wouldn't find in a chain store. When work would allow, I'd attend their weekly open mic. I got up the nerve to participate twice, reading works that I'd written years prior. This was the closest I could get in DC to a slice of Philly. I'd often go alone and sit at the bar. "What's going on, Deesha, same order?" The wait staff knew I only got one thing—fried catfish, collard greens with rice pilaf, lemon sauce on the side. I added chocolate cake sometimes, too, my favorite.

I often wrote in loud spaces like restaurants and subways, influenced by the sound of life around me. Busboys and Poets was such a different world from the White House. It felt like I could step inside and not be in the center of politics anymore.

As I waited for my food, I got my notebook out. I've kept a journal since high school. My thin little five-by-five booklet was wearing on the edges. This booklet would remain my best friend until there were no more pages to fit my musings and ramblings. I was over-whelmed with conflict and felt guilty that I'd been given this amazing job but was unhappy. I felt exposed as an imposter and was wearing it like a bruise. I needed to find a therapist. I wrote:

I have to figure out a way to keep going.
Everything is everywhere and I do not see a way out.

Where are the options? Where is the door?
Please give me the key.

I was confused at what I was even saying or who I
was talking to. Perhaps I should be praying these words
to God instead.

I got the chocolate cake wrapped up to go. I wanted
to get home and lie down before going into work the
next day. I recognized that while circumstances were
changing around my feelings about work, I was also
changing and needed to take responsibility for the ways
in which I allowed myself to be influenced. It felt so
strange. I went home, turned on the series *Big Love*, ate
my cake, and fell asleep being entertained by the drama
of a lily-white, picket-fence polygamous family. Tomorrow was another day.

I knew that I wasn't ready to leave the White House.
I decided to sit tight and keep my ear to the ground
about positions.

One day, I received an email from the First Lady's
Office asking if I'd be interested in a role in the social
office. It was for deputy social secretary under Jeremy,
who was the third Obama social secretary and first
male in the role. He followed Julianna Smoot, who'd
taken over for Desirée Rogers in 2010. I didn't know
him. He was from California via Texas and went back
deep in Democratic politics, most recently as a fundraiser on the 2008 campaign. He'd also served as the
chief of staff in the US embassy in France. I was friends
with plenty of folks in the First Lady's Office, mainly

from doing advance, but overall, I wasn't too hip to how it operated. They were always buttoned up and polished, walking with an aura of authority. Every single one of them. It was mysterious and I was intrigued. I didn't even know how to get to the East Wing where the First Lady's Office was located.

This couldn't have come at a better time, so I started the interview process, which included the First Lady's executive team and some big players in the West Wing. The interviews were standard with questions ranging from my desire to be in the social office and do events to the kind of background skills I had that could benefit the job. I was meeting new people along the way. Since my role in advance wasn't highly visible or senior, many people didn't know me or my background. This was exactly what I wanted, a fresh start and to remain unexposed. I tempered my expectations, though, because there was heavy competition for jobs in the social office.

It wasn't until the final interview with the First Lady herself that things got real. Thankfully I had done a few First Lady trips, so she wasn't a complete stranger, but she also didn't know me well. I was more concerned about my appearance than anything else. I'd deprioritized my work wardrobe since I was on the road so much. It felt like my first day at the internship, when I was worried about what I was going to wear. Michelle Obama was sharp. And I mean, sharp. Hair, nails, shoes, and fits were on point. She was always put together and there was no way that I could walk in there with my same old advance clothes that were comfortable but a little, well, frumpy. I had a few vintage dresses that looked 1970s-glamorous with cloth buttons, high collars, and killer retro patterns. I couldn't afford some of the designer clothes that I saw walking around on the women of the East Wing. And by designer, I'm talking J.Crew and Banana Republic.

I settled on my favorite thrift dress—teal, cinched waist, with buttons down the back. It was a little itchy, but not too bad. It curved in all the right spots and came down to a respectable length, my knees. I got my hair freshly relaxed and my nails done and had one of the interns fix my thinning eyebrows. I searched deep under my desk for heels and settled on a tan pair—something I'd picked up at DSW in my first year at the White House. I had my notes and was as ready as I was going to be.

I walked into her office and she ushered me to sit down on the couch. It didn't feel like a high-pressure interview, although it was. I kept messing with my hands nervously, but I tried to look calm.

"What do you feel you would bring or add to the social office?"

"How is your experience managing a team—because that's a great team over there."

"Do you have any questions for me?"

"No ma'am. I have no questions. Thank you," I concluded before walking out of her office. I went right to the bathroom to take out the papers that I had stuffed under my arms to control nervous sweat, thanking God they hadn't fallen out on the floor when I left the interview. *Whew, I think I did okay? Regardless, it's done.*

The decision didn't take long. The next day I was told I got the position. I was excited to be starting something new, excited that I'd get a badge upgrade and leave Scheduling and Advance. I was sad to be off the road, and I'd miss staying in fancy hotels. Still, I had moved from the office building across from the White House to the East Wing. Greg helped me move and he was more excited than I was—taking pictures of me setting up my new office. "I know you can't get all hype about this, but I will on your behalf," he said while taking some of my belongings out of the box, including photos of my nieces and nephew, framed inspirational quotes, my laptop, photos of my three intern classes that they had made for me, which I proudly displayed on the walls. I'd shared a large office with three people in my previous role and here I'd have my own space, which wasn't quite a private office—more a sectioned-off area in an office shared by two people that connected to Jeremy's big office. It felt surreal to have the ability to walk around the executive mansion unescorted—and this meant I could use the Navy Mess, a dining service in the West Wing run by the US Navy.

I settled into the role and my duties as deputy social secretary. I mainly spent time with the residence staff and colleagues learning about how to execute events. Things like going down to the kitchen to talk to the chef about the considerations they put into state dinner menus, the usher's office on the type of linens, chairs, and tables we had in house, the florist on how she would arrange flowers according to the type of event, calligraphers on their various types of invitations, fonts, and so on. I'd also shadow the social office associates as they put all the particular pieces together on various events. To learn, I ran the easier events like press conferences and sports championships. I was lucky to have run of show templates that allowed me to reference previous events, making the legwork a little easier.

My favorite thing about being the deputy was the ability to invite various community groups, performers, activists, and everyday people to the White House. I was able to share my experience with so many, giving people tickets to tour the garden, trick-or-treat on the lawn at Halloween, or attend one of the extravagant holiday parties. I even got to invite the choir from my high school to perform for the president at a reception, in addition to always making sure Black performers were slated to shine at events. The First Lady encouraged and challenged us to open up the White House so that it truly felt like the People's House. We helped her build a brand of belonging that extended to every person who walked through the doors. This was the core of who she was before she became First Lady: someone who wanted everyone to know that they belonged in these spaces. And that the spaces were created to be enjoyed by those around the world. After all, the White House is a national park and historic landmark paid for by taxpayers. I related closely with this foundation, which reminded me of why her office had been my number one pick as an intern. It took a few months before I started to get comfortable with giving input on events.

The East Wing operated in fast-forward. There were so many events weekly. Every event and every day was different. My role as deputy was sort of undefined and more managerial. It wasn't to be the contact for the events but it also wasn't to be the final decision on them, as that was Jeremy's job. I found the most value adding to the substance and creativity the role allowed. I enjoyed thinking through the performers, food, decorations, and experiences that White House guests could enjoy. *How can we continue to make this White House different? How can we make events memorable while also connecting with their purpose and mission?* I wanted youth, local artists, cultural elements in everything we did—where appropriate, of course. This included marching bands, gospel choirs, art exhibitions, and dancers. These things kept me tied to my roots. I also loved to see the expressions on the faces of those we asked to perform—their amazement at being inside the Obama White House was palpable. The same awe that I had walking in for the first time.

As deputy, I experienced so many entertaining moments that made me shrill in disbelief that this was my actual job. For instance, at my first state dinner in 2014 we hosted President François Hollande of France. A month before his visit, the tabloids broke news of an affair he was having. While this is generally none of my business, Mary J. Blige—thee Mary J. Blige who will make you feel like you personally betrayed someone when she's belting one of her woman-scorned classics—was the entertainment. I both hollered and gasped when she started singing "Not Gon' Cry" in front of President Hollande! Everyone on staff who knew those lyrics from the movie *Waiting to Exhale* had our eyes wide open and I know the president and First Lady—well, at least the First Lady—knew the lyrics, too.

I would stop breathing if you told me to, now you're busy loving someone else

I am 100 percent sure neither Mary nor President Hollande realized what a coincidence it was singing this song amid the scandal. The evening went about as it does, but Mary singing that directly in his face is forever etched in my head.

And then there were events where time slowed down, like the celebration of Black History Month in 2015, when the president and First Lady hosted Sybrina Fulton and Tracy Martin, the parents of Trayvon Martin, a Black teenager who was murdered in 2012. Working with the Office of Public Engagement, we arranged to have someone meet them at the security gate and escort them into the building, where they'd have a private meeting with the president and Mrs. Obama.

I made sure that I was the point on their arrival from our office.

Being at the White House when Trayvon was murdered was hard. I wanted to take to the streets, demand action, cry and rage. I wanted to ask why we weren't doing more. When his killer was acquitted, I felt constrained in how to respond. I had just moved to the First Lady's Office, I worked in one of the most powerful buildings in the world, and still I felt so powerless. It made me question my purpose there. *What change am I making if we can still be killed with no justification?* I went back to my community organizing tactics and decided to gather all the Black First Lady interns to ask how they were truly doing. The interns were close to Trayvon in age. I gathered them in the East Reception Room, which was down the staircase from our offices, and let them just vent and cry. I told them my door would always be open if they needed to talk and process their feelings. They didn't understand why it was all happening and neither did I.

So that day when Ms. Fulton and Mr. Martin walked in the White House doors, I was jolted to a realization that the power I had in that moment was to make them feel welcomed and comfortable; hospitality was all I could offer. They declined water upon entry and thanked me for getting them in the building. A colleague took over their logistics and I went back to my office. I sat there in silence thinking about their pain of losing a son and my privilege of working at the White House. Reconciling this is still hard for me.

Two years away from January 2017, I started to plot my exit. I wanted to ride this wave until they kicked me out, but there wasn't anywhere for me to go from deputy social secretary. Many of my colleagues from both offices had moved on to private companies making twice what they did in government. It's quite an illusion that working at the White House makes you monetarily rich—it's still public service!

For my thirty-seventh birthday in 2015, Jeremy arranged a lovely dinner for just him and me at Le Diplomate, the hip, popular French restaurant on the bustling 14th Street that pays honor to the bistros of Paris Saint-Germain-des-Prés. Everybody who is anybody was clawing to get a reservation at Le Dip. As the social secretary, Jeremy often got a prominent table. Le Dip was also out of my price range, so I was super excited Jeremy was paying. I hadn't wanted to just spring it on him that I was thinking about leaving, so I decided I'd let him know at this dinner. I hadn't thought through how I'd tell the First Lady or our chief of staff. I hadn't thought through my timing or exact reasons for wanting to leave, so for a moment I wondered if it was premature.

As the jazz music played and the bistro lights helped create an elegant atmosphere, I took little bites of my dinner, waiting for the right moment to broach this topic. Every time I was about to, we'd start talking about something else. Finally, there came a moment when we both took a sip of our drinks followed by silence. Except Jeremy jumped in and told me his desire to move back to California and leave the White House, *in the next few months*. My heart was beating fast as I tried to digest the food and his news. Wait, no—I'd thought he was going to stay forever. Before I could even react, he said, "Would you want to be the social secretary?" He cracked a smile, which I was hoping would turn into laughter, indicating his question was clearly a joke. It wasn't.

I responded with extreme laughter. "That job is definitely not for me." Although I had been in the social office for two years, gotten to know Jeremy well, slightly knew Julianna, and had experienced putting White House events together, I still felt there were so many qualities I was missing. All the Obama social secretaries were astute in ways I was not. I wanted to move on from this conversation. It sounded dumb to even entertain the notion of taking his place. Just dumb.

There was more to the job than White House responsibilities. The social secretary had a premier place on the Washington, DC, social scene. From invites to illustrious parties and exclusive dinners to being featured in local press, it was a role that historically sat at the top of the most elite circles of politics and entertainment. Furthermore, the social secretary was seen as the gatekeeper to White House invites, like the coveted state dinners. You were expected to know the political powerhouses, upcoming names, funders, and influential figures around town. Not since the internship had I felt so unqualified for something. There were people who step into Washington with aspirations to be the social secretary, but me? It was comical. Just no.

Jeremy didn't think it was so crazy and told me to think about it. After dinner, I jumped on the Metro, still in disbelief at what had just happened. My house was seven train stops away, and the ride seemed so long as I just kept replaying the conversation over and over. When I got off, I texted my friend Meki's personal phone. She also worked in the administration and checked her phone constantly. Because things always popped up in the world that we'd have to react to, we were always on our phones.

"You up? The craziest thing just happened."

"Uh-oh, call you in a bit."

Meki called ten minutes later and I told her about my crazy conversation with Jeremy. I expected her to laugh with me, but it was complete silence for a few seconds. She actually had a hard time understanding why I wouldn't consider going for the job. She started to list all the reasons I was a good fit:

- institutional knowledge of the White House
- work ethic
- natural desire and ability to bring people together
- entertainment background
- know how to throw a good party
- hospitable

"Why wouldn't you be interested?" This conversation was getting slightly uncomfortable. Having a history of self-doubt makes it hard to hear good things about yourself from someone else. It feels strange.

I sidelined her comments to get the spotlight off me and tried to move on quickly by making a joke. "I don't have social secretary clothes!"

I'm sure Meki thought I was being ridiculous but she humored me. "We can get you clothes."

The next day I went to work as normal with the conversation still on my mind. I was torn over what to do. I knew with Jeremy leaving, I couldn't leave the office with two vacant spots toward the end of the term. I also didn't think I'd want to work under another social secretary, simply because I didn't have the energy to get used to someone else's style. I also knew I couldn't stack up against the talent getting in line for the job. This was going to be competitive. The Philly in me was a natural fighter, but the imposter in me was afraid of losing.

I thought through the scenario of leaving the White House. I had the potential to get a dope job using my credentials and connections. I didn't know what that job was, but perhaps something like a social secretary for a company or international diplomatic protocol officer overseas. I had always wanted to live in another country. Where would I even start this search? It was all daunting to think about.

When I talked about going for the job with trusted colleagues from outside the First Lady's Office, they were like Meki. They had a hard time understanding my aversion to going for it, often repeating the same sentiments as Meki about my qualifications. I knew time was running out to declare my interest as the days passed and Jeremy's pending departure became more widely known. He had let the office and the First Lady know he'd be leaving.

Still unsure if I could pull this off, I made one last

call, to my former colleague Brandon, who'd been a full-time staffer in Scheduling and Advance when I was an intern. When I first met him, I just stared. Honestly, Brandon was one of the most beautiful-looking people I'd ever seen in my life (which seemed hella inappropriate for me to think about as an intern), but that wasn't all—he was funny, kind, and always looking out for me, making sure I understood how to do press on trips. He was younger by five years, but he became a close friend, mentor, and sounding board as my government career began to shape up. He left the White House for a private sector career, but that was derailed by a leukemia diagnosis. He was at the tail end of chemotherapy in the spring of 2015, and while I didn't want to bother him, I wanted his advice. I respected him so much and had already been in talks with him about leaving the White House. I texted his wife and asked if he was up to chatting. She responded, "He has all the time in the world for you." We arranged a call for the next day.

When we got on the phone, I asked about him over and over while apologizing for the call. "Stoooooooop! What's up?" he said. I proceeded to tell him about the open social secretary position and how I was thinking about going for it. While I can't recall all the words, I remember him mustering up enough energy to say as boldly as possible, "You have to do it. Keep me posted on how it goes."

I made it known that week that I would like the role. Ultimately, I didn't want to regret not trying. I didn't want to end my career five years in wondering how things could have been. I had visions of being laughed out of interviews, but I prayed incessantly for just the courage to not give up.

There was no time to even think of what it all meant because immediately, my calendar started to fill up with interviews. Immediately! Like, holy shit! What had I done? My world started spinning. I was bouncing from the executive office building on the complex grounds to the West Wing to the East Wing to coffee shop meetings to lunches at Hamilton Restaurant down the street from the White House. Every single day after I expressed my interest in the role, I made sure my hair, nails, and outfits were together. I stopped wearing flats as much as I could and would change into my heels a few blocks before getting to the entry gate for work. I wanted to be seen as a lady boss who could wear heels and run shit—I also wanted to look fabulous doing it. Flat shoes may convey that I didn't care about appearance or style, and although naturally those things weren't a priority for me, this wasn't the time to let that be known. I was being watched closely. I felt silent pressure from senior colleagues who were invested in the person who would eventually end up with this role. But the most pressure came internally, from myself.

Unlike the internship, where I was competing with thousands who applied, I was informed that only a small number of applicants were vying for this job. I knew some of the people and they were legit, poised, and what I'd consider a perfect fit. Once I found this out, my imposter syndrome started to show itself. It felt awful because it fed the justification I gave myself for not wanting to go for this job in the first place. It sparked paranoia that every little thing I did would be watched and scrutinized. I did my best to mask it by acting bubbly, cheery, and applying an unhealthy dose of toxic positivity. We all do this, saying *It's all good* when really, it's not. We put a sunny filter on everything, instead of just admitting that shit is sometimes really messed up or scary. We're more digestible when we are upbeat, but at some point it becomes toxic to keep smiling, nodding, and pretending.

There was a slight performance element to being the social secretary, which made the interview process seem like an audition. I'd never been one to have stage fright, I told myself. I could get through it. An audition, yes.

I was asked by a colleague if there was anything in my past that would reflect badly on the office of the president. I was confused by the question but understood why they were asking. No one wanted something unsavory to come out in the press that would surprise the White House. At the end of the day, they were doing their job.

While I am completely comfortable with my decision to have an abortion, it remains one of the most divisive and politicized issues of our time. I let them know I'd written about mine in 2003 for the *Philadelphia Daily News*. They said that was fine. I slid in my eviction, bad credit (which was repaired by then), and some hip-hop articles that spoke very clearly about misogyny and sex. Part of me hoped these things would disqualify me, so I could give validation to my imposter syndrome of not being deserving and go on with my life. Let me off the hook for this important role that I wasn't sure I deserved or could get, but now wanted. That's not what happened, though, because none of those things mattered.

Several weeks had gone by since the start of the interview process. I had been working hard on a Power-Point to present to the First Lady that focused on the final two years of the presidency. It was very detailed, with ideas such as a full HBCU marching band performing on the lawn, a thank-you event for all Obama appointees, a Greek step show, a hip-hop education day, and more. There was also a list of performers that we hadn't yet seen on the slide. Folks like Drake, Taylor Swift, Jay-Z, and the Roots. I wanted to bring in more DJs and guest chefs, and have more interactive experiences on the lawn while the weather could accommodate. I included ways we could give memorable experiences to our guests—not just them attending events. The presentation didn't speak to the traditional events like state dinners, because those were built in, automatic in some ways. It was seven pages long and I was damn proud of it. I printed out two copies for my final interview with the First Lady, as well as my résumé. This was a higher-stakes interview than the one for deputy two years prior.

You could still smell the relaxer on my hair. All the running around DC during this process plus maintaining my job really brought my roots out so I'd had a fresh do done the day before. I had also taken my fake-gold earrings and faux-diamond necklace to a jeweler at the mall to see if they could make them look less…fake? I made sure my nails were done in a neutral color and although DC was warming up, I could still hear both my grandmothers' voices telling me to put something on them legs. My nerves were high, but I felt ready.

The First Lady had just finished a meeting and I was up next. Her scheduler called me in. I stood waiting as the previous meeting-goers poured out; some colleagues walked past me and whispered "Good luck," while others didn't make eye contact. Once I was ushered in, I sat down. She asked first how I was doing, just as she had for the deputy role. I wanted to scream, *I'M FIGHT-ING FOR MY LIFE OUT HERE MA'AM*, but instead I answered a very polite, "I'm doing great. Thank you so much for asking. How are you?" Like she was going to sit and tell me how she actually was doing, as if we were friends. "Oh, I can't complain," she said.

I handed her the purple folder, which had a smudge on it from the lotion I'd just put on my hands. I didn't want to walk in there ashy, not with a Black First Lady who definitely knew what ashy looked like!

She asked me what it was in the folder. I let her know it was my résumé and some ideas I had for how I'd approach being the social secretary. She put it down before even opening it. *Well, that isn't a good sign, is it?!* I didn't panic. She started talking about the confidence needed to do the job and if I had it. The First Lady had this way of asking the one question that you weren't prepared for. This happened all the time, even though we staffers did our best to figure out what she'd ask. I swallowed the question, confused how to answer, then pulled my chin up a little bit and took a breath—but not too long that she would interpret that as a no, which wouldn't be entirely inaccurate.

I cannot lie, but I also cannot throw this opportunity away. I was six years deep into working at the White House. Whether she'd observed it herself, heard it through the grapevine, or was aware of the feeling of lack we Black women often experience, it was out on the table, front and center. I felt embarrassed at that moment. I didn't think anyone else had noticed my struggles but me, not realizing that they manifested in unhealthy ways in my interactions and moods. I thought I masked them well, but I didn't. For those who have these brutal battles with confidence, we spend a lot of time covering up the issue instead of fixing it. This can go on for years and years before we realize that there's more to it and it's wasted effort to keep pretending.

With the First Lady sitting across from me, both of us with crossed legs, I cupped my knee nervously and replied, "Yes, I have the confidence to do this job."

She nodded before saying a list of positive qualities she saw in me, many of the same things I'd heard from Meki the first night Jeremy approached me about the job. The First Lady said she believed in me, but in order to succeed in this job, I had to believe in *myself* because this was the last two years and she wanted to do as much as we could for as many people as we could.

She also mentioned that this was a highly visible role where people would be asking for things constantly, so I would have to set boundaries and know how to say no with a smile. I took this as a directive that I needed to get it together quickly—there wasn't time for my confidence to catch up. She then congratulated me on being the next White House social secretary.

Here comes the brand new flava in ya ear.

It was so fitting to have Craig Mack's song hit me as I walked into work the next day. I received a mountain of congratulations from my co-workers. I was still in disbelief and didn't have that much time to celebrate, as I was in charge of a gospel concert that night featuring Aretha Franklin, Pastor Shirley Caesar, Tamela Mann, Michelle Williams, the Morgan State University Choir, and more. It was a regular collaboration we had with the local PBS station to broadcast concerts from the White House. This would be my last event as a deputy. As the president came to meet the First Lady on the State Floor to enter the concert, he saw me and yelled, "Deesha, I hear some congratulations are in order," before giving me a side hug. I said thank you and started to brief them on the logistics of the night.

I had climbed from an intern to this senior position in a matter of six years. I went from not knowing Washington, DC, at all to being at the epicenter of social status where I gained a lot of new best friends who wanted to get access to the president and First Lady. Some of the influential guards in Washington, primarily older white women, would try to slip me their used designer purses and clothes as gifts to help me in my new role, they'd say. These are people who didn't know I existed a year ago and wouldn't care about me if not for my new shiny title. I was always polite declining their hand-me-downs, but accepted all the fancy party invites. I knew this time would be fleeting so I enjoyed myself as much as I could. Even when an elder DC socialite came up to me and said, "Did you mean to paint your nails blue?" I just laughed. Yes, lady, I did. I realized I'd aced the audition and moved on to the performance.

Stepping into the role helped quiet the imposter voice...a little. It was not defeated, but the loud roar turned into a soft whisper, allowing me to proudly hear and own my part in a life I'd earned. When we silence the imposter, we release the limitations that bound our curiosity and creativity. I found myself walking a little bit taller, saying thank you to compliments without a long explanation to follow, and seeing myself as a leader. My fists unballed, releasing some (not all) of the anger, frustration, and fight I carried around in defense of myself, my character, my education, my gender, and my race. Some, but not all, because the testing of my patience and character continued. I had nothing to prove externally and everything to prove internally. I was deserving of all the good things.

It'd be misleading for me to act like this promotion of a lifetime was the cure I needed; nor do I want to suggest that it takes a high achievement like this to see yourself as worthy. Job titles come and go, as do opportunities, but the journey to get there reveals the truths that we need. The truths that tell us we are capable of more than we can conceive of. The journey provides you the proof you need to unlearn the unhealthy things you've digested about yourself.

Shortly after I became social secretary, a young Black woman from Philadelphia became an intern in the Office of the First Lady. A colleague who supervised her reached out and said, "Hey, our intern is from Philadelphia and she mentioned you as the inspiration for why she applied for the internship. She'd love to meet you if you can spare a moment."

I could spare a moment. I had a meeting like this once every two weeks as I kept my door open for interns and was a speaker for the intern class every semester.

When the intern walked in, we immediately started busting it up about Philly. She recognized my Phillies and Sixers décor on the wall and smiled. "How can I help you?" I asked her.

Her answer is one I'll never forget. Her voice got a little shaky: "You are the reason I applied for this internship. Watching your journey—a girl from Philly—gave me the confidence to say I could do this, too. You are authentically yourself without forgetting about the community and where you came from. I just wanted to say thank you for all you do for me and Black girls like me. You are doing it!"

The gravity of this moment hit and hit hard. I didn't tear up, but I wanted to because without knowing me personally, she knew my struggle.

"I may be the reason you applied," I told her, "but you are the reason you're here. This is a manifestation of all good things and it doesn't stop here. Being yourself is not easy, especially in places that have never recognized greatness out of someone that carries themselves as we do. I can promise you that this all took a while."

We both laughed because I didn't have to say anything more. She understood exactly what I meant.

CHAPTER 6

The Steep Cost of Being Yourself

My first food service job was at age seventeen in the mall at the sandwich bakery Au Bon Pain. It was there that I started to understand the ways in which my identity as a Black woman was weaponized in the workplace. I was closing the shift with the store manager and another worker when it was realized that money in the register didn't add up to the orders we had taken in from customers. As I was wiping the counters off with the very strong bleach rag we used, I could sense someone was standing close to me.

"Were you on the register all day today?" my manager asked.

"There were three of us since opening."

"It's $50 short. Do you know anything about that?"

His tone got more aggressive, almost like a snarl.

Before I could answer, he proceeded to tell me that I acted like I didn't want to be there and had a bad attitude with customers. Only half of this was true: I definitely didn't want to be there. I kept to myself and didn't socialize and joke around with him or the other workers, which was seen as having an attitude problem. I didn't get to answer before he decided to write me up for being "insubordinate." As he came out from the back office to where I was now cleaning the glass windows that sat above the food stations, he told me to sign my write-up and flippantly asked again, "And you don't know anything about the missing money?"

I replied no, left the unsigned paperwork on his desk, finished cleaning the counter, and started to gather my things to leave. It was such an accusatory question. The damage that it caused was great and stuck with me for several years. I left questioning myself and the missing money. Did I punch in the wrong amount during or after a transaction? The other worker, a white girl who got along well with the manager, asked if she could head home. "Sure, see you tomorrow," he said. She was at the register with me the entire time and never got asked about the money. She also was his after-work drinking buddy who could do no wrong. This situation has repeated itself under different circumstances in various jobs.

At the time, I internalized this treatment and thought it was isolated to just me. There was no social media back then or articles that chronicle the shared similarities of experiences among Black people, women, and especially Black women, which meant there also was no accountability. I felt I was being targeted, but never had the language or courage to vocalize it and take action. This grew and grew and grew as I got older and obtained more professional experience. I felt like the biggest failure when I made any mistakes. As a Black woman I felt put down, as if the way I acted—just by being myself—was harmful.

When I got promoted to White House social secretary, I hit the ground running. I really didn't know how deep the pressure, anxiety, and fear of being in the role would go because I was really excited about the innovative and entertaining ways the house could open up more. But no matter how hard I tried to push the narrative out of my head, I couldn't escape that I wasn't the model fit. The constant thoughts would play on loop in my head.

Since I can remember, I have watched white men and women be afforded praise for their leadership, when in the next breath I or other Black women were labeled uncooperative and unprofessional. Instead of rejecting this difference as racial aggression, I was convinced, *Maybe it actually is me? How can I be more likeable?*

Ever since my interviews to move to the East Wing, I'd worked pretty hard to keep my issues hidden. I also knew that my newfound position was being watched with admiration by young politicos, especially women, who had dreams of being social secretary or working in the White House someday. I was often conflicted over how much of myself I should show at work. I'd never been good at code-switching (the act of alternating between two different personas according to the environment you're in)—it seems like so much effort. I did a bit here and there, and it was exhausting. Black people are experts at this. We often feel the pressure to code-switch to get along and be respected by others. Thankfully more and more of us are divorcing from the need to appease others or live up to the ideals and standards of non-Black people.

There's a population of Black people who see code-switching as necessary in order to move up the social, economic, and professional ladders. Many are too afraid to ruffle feathers in fear of being typecast or seen as someone who doesn't play nicely in the sandbox. Code-switching could have been the secret sauce to being called a team player or being invited to certain parties. It's something many of us are pushed into unknowingly since birth. It's a way of not going batshit crazy in a workplace or a way to climb the ladder for more financial security. While I hate this in all its forms, I do understand how Black people are stuck in this matrix. It's a form of survival.

However, I couldn't shy away from being myself, especially in the White House. I entered the political world as a thirty-one-year-old intern. I was too mature in my life to figure out how to be someone else—but also too insecure not to question if being me was okay.

I didn't want to compromise the parts of myself that made other people uncomfortable because I didn't operate in the confines of the box they built for me. I wasn't going to take my nose ring out, nor was I going to wear a weave, nor was I willing to be quiet when I had questions or concerns. I had enough to do and frankly, the energy to twist myself into a hundred pieces to appease the masses wasn't there. People had to work out their own insecurities, assumptions, and conscious biases. If I was a trigger or a catalyst to ego and power, that was not my bag to carry. If I gave that power over to others, I'd look in the mirror and actually see an imposter, someone I had been fast running from.

Working that philosophy out in real time sparked a wave of unnecessary distractions. One of them was tone-policing: being told that my voice, when I'm giving a particular comment or opinion, is too loud, too strong, too bold, too brash, or too harsh, and that the tone has offended other people.

This rhetoric against Black women in the workplace, whether we are running major corporations, running a country, or working at a café like Au Bon Pain, is exhausting and insufferable. Rarely were my conversations about the matter at hand; instead they involved someone's feelings about me. This happens all the time in the workplace, and there is never accountability for those who commit these offenses, except more blame on us as Black women insinuating that we're being "sensitive" or "taking it the wrong way" when we are upset by being seen as threatening because of who we are.

To a certain group of people in this world, I was someone who was never meant to be seen in a position of power or authority. I, like many who aren't white men, have to fight, climb, and overcome barriers that have been present since the beginning of time. We as Black women know we are leaders, we know we hold power, but so much time, energy, and money are spent telling us otherwise. It's about the power that others, who see us as inferior, wield over us. So we spend a lot of time spent chasing the dream of overall acceptance, when just being ourselves isn't enough.

I wasn't fooled by my title or the prestige of my role; I knew what I was up against so I acted accordingly, turning my fight mode on full blast.

Human beings in stressful, complicated, threatening, or controversial situations typically have four modes of responding: fight, flight, freeze, or fawn. *Fight* is a physical response. You may tense up your shoulders, make fists, bite down on your teeth, or cry with emotional anger. This is your body preparing to defend itself. *Flight* urges you to get out of Dodge quickly. Often this looks like avoidance: a lack of eye contact, leaving the room, or hands and legs fidgeting. *Freeze* is exactly what it sounds like: You feel stuck, numb, sometimes physically unable to move to flee a situation that's causing you discomfort. Your body is not sure how to react, so it feels a little suffocated. Lastly, *fawn* is usually a secondary option when one of the other three doesn't help you feel better. Fawn is going to the extreme to people-please as a method of avoidance. This looks like always expressing agreement, even when you disagree, and constantly putting others' needs before your own as a way to navigate a situation by taking the path of least resistance—faking it until you make it out of the distressing or threatening situation.

In my new role at the White House, I was firmly planted in fight mode, sometimes dipping my toe into fawn.

I knew that in order to survive, I had to hold tight to pieces of me that wouldn't budge. I was aware that this could garner me a reputation—one that I still carry. A reputation that confirms what the world thinks of Black women in general, no matter how many degrees we hold, promotions we obtain, or problems we solve. This reputation is that we are combative, not a team player, and difficult.

I finally gave up and stopped caring, really. I accepted that these labels would follow me throughout my life. I decided to embrace them. I had to divest from the need to seek and want approval. I made peace with this and it became a challenging comfort and palpable joy for me to stand ten toes down on my authenticity. It helped me sleep better at night and smile in the mirror when I woke up. Finding this peace remains the most solid part of me. At the same time, the loss of belonging flickered into a functional depression. I kept doing my job day in and day out but felt sad and just down.

I always lived in conflict with who I was, who people wanted me to be, who I was becoming, and what I was doing. I didn't have that foundational grounding that seals in a secure sense of self. I only knew how to survive, and to my credit, I thought I was doing a pretty good job. So I decided to stop trying to look for compromises in my conversations, clothes, thoughts, and everything else. All I could think was that every self-help anything I'd ever bought, listened to, or digested owed me a refund because it was not fun just "being myself."

Your people will find you. Catchy self-help-book-ish advice like that wasn't proving true in my experience. As many times as I've heard this, it was never comforting to me. I'm impatient, and hearing that in my bout of loneliness didn't soothe my need for community and friendship in workspaces. I had a multitude of follow-up questions, like *When will they find me? And will it be soon? Will these be people who accept me just how I am, with flaws and all? People who'll be friends without judgment or competition? Where are they?*

Feeling lonely sometimes was partially my own doing. A way of protecting myself or not exposing myself too much to people. In spite of this, I have always found my people, like at the White House when I became close to a group of Black women who were navigating their own journeys. We often supported each other, and many of those friendships are still intact today. I am so thankful, but still recognize that authenticity is a hard concept to digest. I had to accept that it has the potential to make others uncomfortable. And I had to sometimes ask myself: Was it really worth it then? I questioned whether I was a good, loving, fun enough person that others actually would want to have around. Honestly, if the answer was no, I'd have to move on and be okay with it.

The world has cashed in on selling us ways to be our authentic selves while carelessly advising that we show up as such in spaces, like work, that aren't ready to receive all that we are. With the new, shiny focus on mental health these days, there are hundreds of apps, billboards, clothing companies, and streaming shows focused on selling positivity. It's genius marketing that works. I feel GREAT when I read inspirational quotes like *be the change you want to see,* or when I meditate, but that feeling fades as the day goes on, and I'm right back where I started—questioning myself and who I am. The environments encouraging us to be ourselves are sometimes the same ones pushing back and punishing us for *being* ourselves. My job environment said, *Come as you are! Just be yourself!* But then I could be reprimanded for speaking up too forcefully in a meeting, or be made to feel like an outcast because I didn't fit in personality-wise or with the hobbies and interests of my co-workers, for example. Someone, anyone—make it make sense!

Sometimes being yourself is just, well, hard. Humans crave community, inclusion, friendship, and companionship, so we often subtly mold ourselves to fit in and get just that. I believe that most people don't know how to be themselves because we want to stay in the circle of social community. I get it. I've experienced it.

But we have to get comfortable with *not* belonging sometimes. Continuing to give power to the opinions of others does nothing but cause you a cycle of anxiety that will infest every facet of your life until it becomes a reality that you don't even realize is there. As I get older, this gets easier for me to manage and recognize, but despite the tough exterior I display, the strong warrior shield of independence I wear, and the constant pats on the back that I'm giving myself, exclusion sucks and still doesn't feel good.

To be clear, I knew that I was not above growth and accountability. There were some rough edges to me that needed a little filing, some smoothing over—especially as I began to climb the ranks at the White House. I was eager and excited to learn how to bob, weave, and maneuver in the uncharted waters of government. I knew I had to adjust part of my conduct and behavior—not for respectability, politics, or acceptance, but for communication and effectiveness at the job I was appointed to do.

It took me a while to be comfortable with isolation, a reputation for rebellion, and figuring out how to minimize the power that I let others have over me to silence myself. I am very encouraged that my nieces and the rest of Gen-Z are growing up having more autonomy over their voices and actions. While they still face oppressive systemic and institutional structures that thrive off feeding doubt, they are less afraid, they call things out, and they work to define their own pipelines of success. I'm not sure why this is, but I do see the rise in our ability to connect through social media and technology as a factor. Gen-Z has realized that organizing is powerful and there is strength in numbers. They have endless amounts of information at their fingertips from all over the world, giving them alternative perspectives that allow them to form their own opinions and conclusions. They discovered there are other ways to live, to thrive, and to succeed, and they have witnessed the generations before them, including their parents, make mistakes that they do their best to avoid.

Older generations have a lot to learn from Gen-Z and the way they operate. There's a lot to harvest from watching them maneuver. The way they mobilize around their rights in the workplace and focus on taking care of communities through mutual aid campaigns. Increasing numbers of high school seniors are breaking the stale formula of the "graduation to college to the workforce" pipeline, and are deciding to do other things, or do the same but differently.

Young people have been an inspiring force by showcasing another possible way of life. A new way comes with more freedom and control over ourselves, leaving little space for the insecurities of others to take root in us.

Learning to be yourself isn't easy because our selves are constantly shifting as we evolve. We often miss these changes within because we're busy worrying about what's happening in the outside world, how we're perceived, and what we need to fix about ourselves. Living and embracing our changing authentic selves becomes secondary.

There is a divine, welcoming way for you to walk

through this life as yourself. And there will be a community there to receive all that you are and all that you bring. It's worth it. You *will* find your people just by being yourself. But in this process you just may also learn that *everyone* isn't meant to be one of those people.

CHAPTER 7

Peace Be With You.
And Also.

re you okay?"
Somehow I was able to get out a very faint,
"Yes, I'm fine—thanks," as I hovered over the toilet in
the upstairs bathroom of the East Wing. It was 3:00 a.m.
and I had been vomiting for a few minutes, just like I
had been every morning for the past few days. I grabbed
a small piece of tissue to wipe my mouth, immediately
went to the sink to brush my teeth, and then returned to
my office to lie down before sunrise in just a few hours.
My head hit the pillow on my twin-size, navy-blue
blow-up mattress that fit perfectly between my door
and my desk. I had a full-size sheet to lie on and a small
quilted blanket to keep me warm from the breezy draft
that always found its way into my office. With eyes still
a little wet from vomiting, I kept repeating a prayer to

God, *Please just get me through this day. Help me be strong. Help me feel better. Please just get me through this day.*

The first official visit of Pope Francis to the White House was happening in just a few hours, and clearly God didn't want me to be sick to greet the most high of his men on earth, right? If anything, this was the prayer he needed to be listening to. To prepare for the twelve thousand people expected on the White House lawn, trying to get a glimpse of this iconic religious figure and the Obamas, there were massive barriers up and scanning machines surrounding the gates on all sides. The White House slots were ticketed, but people wanted to be the first to get in and secure a space, so Lafayette Park, across the street from the mansion, had campers out from the night before. Even if people didn't have a ticket, they stood for hours overnight with photos and rosaries just to be part of the experience.

Since I had to be up at 6:00 a.m. to start the preparations for the visit, I'd opted to sleep in my office, afraid that trying to commute from my apartment twenty minutes away was too much of a risk on a day like today. We had a full shower in our communal bathroom, and my office had enough privacy that I could get ready. I wouldn't have been able to sleep at home anyway, so I chose to be where I was around the clock if needed. I'd have to skip listening to my ratchet hype morning music and substitute some gospel, but I needed Jesus that morning so the switch was A-okay.

September 23, 2015, was a date etched into the White House calendar for months before I even took up the social secretary role. Jeremy and I had a running joke that he left just in time. The fall madness began with the papal visit, a state dinner, and Halloween festivities before we then springboarded into the holiday season full of decorations, tours, and parties. My nerves had been shot for about two months leading up to this day. Anything pertaining to the outdoor conditions was an automatic stressor for me. I kept the Weather Channel on the TV in my office, browser on my computer, and tab on my BlackBerry, refreshing about three times a day. One of the most gut-wrenching things about being the social secretary is making a weather call to move an event inside when it's meant to be outdoors, on display to the public. This was only the third pope to ever visit the White House, and it was all happening under my watch. *Jesus, you got me on this weather too, right, homie?* I edited the prayer just a little as I stared at the weather scan.

I was also terrified of an impromptu protest breaking out on the lawn or, even worse, a streaker running naked with a political message painted on their body in the hope of getting press attention. It honestly would have been the event for nationally televised foolishness with Pope Francis, President Obama, and a massive amount of national and international press on-site. Our office worked closely with the White House Visitors Office, which was charged with ticketing, entry, and crowd logistics on contingency plans if a protest did break out, but the thought was still circling in my mind nonstop. There was an expected high level of pressure, with all the excitement and unpredictability at play.

The trembles in my body, goose bumps on my skin, and irregular heartbeats communicating the high anxiety that was filling my body greatly affected my sleep, appetite, focus, and information processing time. My mood changed minute by minute. My exhaustion manifested itself into eating chicken fingers and fries from the Navy Mess almost every single night for a month. Add to that two barbecue sauces. Oh, and I'd just gotten the news right before this monumental visit that I was six weeks pregnant.

"A Rookie Brings Her Skills to the 'Super Bowl' of Social Planning." This headline published September 20, 2015, in the *New York Times* was accompanied by a picture of me in an intense audience stare, standing next to a social office colleague at an event in the East Room. The article went on to explain that I had only been on the job four months and questioned whether I was ready for the next week of White House festivities, which started with the pope's state visit, continued with the state visit of President Xi, and closed out with the United Nations General Assembly, where over 150 world leaders would descend upon New York City and the president and First Lady would host multiple events.

Lines in print about me for the world to see in one of the nation's most prestigious publications, "a community college graduate who became White House intern at the relatively advanced age of 31" and "Ms. Dyer's résumé is a big departure from those of previous White House social secretaries, who from Letitia Baldrige in the Kennedy administration to Capricia Marshall in the Clinton administration typically inhabited the world of their guests," sent a bat signal to my imposter syndrome to come out of hiding.

But there was no room at that exact point. No room for doubt, insecurities, pity, or wondering if I was good enough. There was no time. My world was spinning and the very last thing I was concerned with was an article reminding me that I am a girl from Philly with a community college degree who wrote about hip-hop and didn't move in Washington circles. Instead, I focused on squeezing in hobbies and positive coping mechanisms like therapy, exercising, dance class, writing, and cooking. Those things gave me energy for the tough workdays. I was amped up to make these events flawless and perfect. It motivated me to prove people wrong.

I had prepared for this special week for months. In addition to our two- to three-hour weekly planning meetings, briefing updates with the president and First Lady, multiple edits to the timeline, and walkthroughs of the spaces, I had all my outfits ready—a tea-length burgundy dress that covered my arms and knees in line with attire and decorum protocol for the pope, a bright custom-made gown with a silk shawl for the China state dinner, and three thrift dresses with cardigan sweaters for New York—and I had breakfast and snack bars for quick meals throughout the day, hair and makeup appointments lined up, a battery pack charged for my phone, and two gallons of water in my office stocked up for hydration. My adrenaline matched the pace of my nerves, but I knew that I'd done all I could to make this a memorable, remarkable week...and not get fired!

Luckily for me, the individual responsibilities of the visits were shared by a multitude of extremely talented, experienced colleagues—some who had institutional knowledge from working multiple state visits through various presidential administrations. I had a team of six in the social office that took on individual responsibilities for the visit while checking in with me on the details. In addition to us there were the US Secret Service, which led all protection details; the US State Department, which served as our protocol and diplomacy experts; the White House Visitors Office, which worked on crowd maintenance, entry, and control; the White House Military Office, which handled the pageantry and procedures for events; the White House Communications Agency, focusing on the official microphones, speakers, and overall sound; the National Security Council, helping us with the national security and policy direction; and the Executive Residence, which included the chefs, butlers, housekeepers, florists, calligraphers, and others. These various White House departments across the East and West Wings served in support with guest lists, staffing, and more. The most sophisticated and diplomatic chaos I'd ever seen. And I was somehow in charge of it all.

Pope Francis was fairly new to the papacy, having just been elected in 2013. He took over for Pope Benedict XVI, who'd held the position for eight years, and in his third year of the papacy visited President George W. Bush at the White House. This would be Francis's first visit to the United States as pope. Add that to a popular and charismatic president, and the result was a meeting of the minds that would be watched around the world.

September is also the livest month in DC for Black people in politics. The weekend before the pope's visit, the Annual Legislative Conference produced by the Congressional Black Caucus took place. The CBC is made up of Black House and Senate members from Capitol Hill. There are a multitude of conferences during the day focused with political agendas, and even more brunches, parties, happy hours, and black-tie dinners where folks would stunt and stroll with their peers. I had attended these events for several years, since being hired at the White House in 2010, but the role of social secretary came with an all-access badge to all the top-tier events. I liked acting like I didn't care about the events, but that was a lie. I made sure I was seen, heard, and photographed looking fly at as many events as possible. I was also, technically, single at the time, living by myself, and CBC weekend provided opportunities to be not-so-single. I also decided to use that Saturday as a day off from planning the state visits. I wanted to party without stress for one day, so I told the team that we'd regroup on Sunday.

Fiola Mare, a swanky Italian restaurant on the Georgetown waterfront, was the first stop for the weekend. There was a brunch scheduled and I was meeting my homegirl Addie there. She was Black, hailed from Atlanta, and worked in communications at the White House. She and I had gotten real close over the years, and she was excited to unwind as she'd just orchestrated an *Essence* magazine spread a few months earlier titled, "29 Powerful Black Women Who Call the Shots in the Obama Administration." It was a beautiful photographic spread of our faces and small blurbs about our jobs.

"What time are you getting there?" I asked.

"Probably around noon," she responded. We agreed to meet right behind the check-in desk.

The food at Fiola Mare was known to be delicious and pricey, so I was more than delighted not to pay for anything, as it was a catered affair sponsored by a company. My bright floral dress was ready to go, along with heels that I would carry in my bag and change into after I got off the bus that took me to the restaurant. The dress was a little snug around the belly—more than usual. I was extremely tired, but chalked it up to the intense workweek. I felt slightly off—not enough to keep me from eating at Fiola Mare, but enough to spend the $25 on an Uber to get to Georgetown.

Immediately upon arriving at the restaurant, I swapped my sneakers for heels and headed to the check-in desk. CBC also drew beautiful men to town, and I looked on point just in case God decided to bless me that particular afternoon! I wasn't aggressively looking for a man, but I was looking.

Addie arrived before me. As I was waiting for the registration clerk to find my name on the guest list, the sudden smell of seafood, perfume, cologne, and potential bad decisions hit me. I felt a little nauseous. I told Addie I'd be right back and ran to the bathroom in anticipation of throwing up. False alarm—nothing came up. She got me a seltzer water with lemon and I sipped on that for a few minutes while exchanging pleasantries and laughs over a hip-hop soundtrack in the background.

"Girl, you okay?" Addie asked.

"Yes, I'll be fine. I'm just so tired and it's messing with my stomach."

"I understand that."

I downed two glasses of water and with my appetite finally back, I excused myself from a conversation to find the waiters passing around canapés including some type of bread with olives, bacon-wrapped scallops, and ceviche tostada, which I beelined to get. It looked so good and refreshing. I was starved and very unladylike and put one entirely in my mouth. I chewed it up, swallowed the first piece—it was delicious. Kept chewing, went to swallow the second piece, and the unsettled feeling came back to my stomach. I felt it coming back up. I went to the bathroom, which wasn't far, and threw up the canapé and water. When I was done, I leaned on the inside of the stall door to wipe my face off while searching frantically for a mint. I washed my hands and decided to leave. I would text Addie later.

She was right outside the bathroom looking for me. "My nerves are all over the place. I'll just see you at the dinner gala later," I said as I made my exit.

My dress for the black-tie gala Phoenix gala was already too small, with buttons down the front that buckled a bit around my mid-back. As long as it could close, I was fine, but I planned to stop by Macy's anyway just to see what was on sale. After getting sick at brunch and feeling like a stuffed sausage in the dress I wore there, I was focused on finding something else for the gala. I took a cab to Macy's in downtown DC. There were six hours until the gala, time enough to get a new dress, take a nap, shower, eat (no one actually *ate* the dinner), get ready, and head out for the night.

I had been pregnant before, as I mentioned earlier. I'd even publicly written about it for a local publication years back, but I didn't exactly remember what it felt like. I was in an "entanglement" of sorts, but not a formal relationship, and I wasn't on birth control, so it was definitely possible. Throwing up worried me. I could count on one hand how many times I'd actually vomited in my life. Though I felt pretty sure I wasn't pregnant this time around, I wanted to get the thought out of my head that maybe I could be. I already had enough on my mind. There was no room to contemplate a pregnancy, too.

I went over to a CVS two blocks from Macy's. A red-and-white cab dropped me off out front, and I ran to the feminine hygiene aisle and grabbed a test. I didn't even want to wait until I got home to take the test. I was eager to stop thinking about it. My stomach had settled except the flutters over the outcome of the test. I'd cut through Macy's plenty of times on my way home from work, as the department store is connected to the Metro train, so I walked swiftly inside and headed straight for the bathrooms. Beautiful crystal bowls and matching plates and napkins whirled by me, lavishly made beds calling my name with perfectly plush pillows and down feather comforters. I hurried past them, hoping I was moving fast enough that no one would see me—DC being the small place that it is and with CBC happening nearby, there was a good chance that I'd run into someone on my way to the bathroom looking completely disheveled. I picked up speed.

The bathroom was empty. I ripped open the box and peed on the stick, the sound echoing in the vacant space. I placed the test on top of the silver metal trash bin for feminine products and waited. Results were guaranteed in three minutes, but thirty seconds seemed like three minutes. I looked—nothing yet. I waited another minute and looked again. One line had appeared, which meant the test was active. Very faintly, the second line appeared.

I told myself, *It's very faint and not the best lighting in here*, so I waited another minute before I picked up the test and held it to the light.

Shit! What? *No. This can't be.*

But it could be, and it was. Shit.

There was no way I could go to the gala with this news. I was frozen. Unsure of what to do next. I believed the test, but I also wanted a confirmation. This was undoubtedly the very worst time of my life for a pregnancy. I exited the stall and felt tears welling in my

eyes, stinging as I washed my hands. I looked up at the
bathroom mirror and they fell one by one. I was in a
Macy's bathroom stall, crying, a pregnancy stick in my
hand. I felt defeated, overwhelmed, like a failure, and
alone.

After I dried my hands, I slid my sunglasses over
my eyes, hoping again that I wouldn't run into anyone
I knew, especially someone from a press outlet. I had
this whole scenario in my head that a reporter would
stop me to say hi, and the pregnancy test would fall out
of my purse, and the news would end up in *Playbook*,
the daily sightings blog from the newspaper *Politico*. The
headline would read, "Black, Unmarried, Single, Community College Graduate and Senior Aide to the First
Black First Lady of the United States of America Seen
Wailing in a Public Bathroom Holding a Positive Pregnancy Test." A long headline, I know, but it encapsu-
lated everything I felt about myself in that moment. I
felt reduced down to just that.

The narrative I had been running from was haunting me, one that feeds a core element of imposter
syndrome—feeling like a fraud. I had painted this picture of myself, now that I'd risen through the ranks at
the White House, that I was responsible, made good
decisions, and was a leader. This latest life event seemed
to prove all at once that this new image of myself was a
lie. The center of my concern wasn't my health—it was
how I'd be perceived, talked about, and judged. Doubt-
ing myself caused me to deprioritize my health, a chilling and dangerous side effect to imposter syndrome.

Instead, I wondered how long I could hide this from everyone so they didn't think I was unfit for the job of social secretary—so they wouldn't think of me the thoughts I'd secretly been battling about with myself. How was I going to get through the upcoming week of monster events like nothing at all was happening?

I heard someone else enter the bathroom and panicked, the thought of my shame and electrifying headlines spinning through my mind. I grabbed my things and left as the other person entered the toilet stall.

Everything felt out of my control. I didn't know what to do. I'd let everyone down, from the president and First Lady to my friends, family, community of mentees, and all those who'd told me I was inspirational and that they looked up to me.

Dazed as I got on the train to return home, I texted Addie and a few other friends that I wasn't going to the dinner gala. I got home and sat down on the couch, three things on my mind: (1) getting to the doctor for a confirmation, (2) the safest, soonest, and quietest way to have an abortion, and (3) how to get through the next week with all of this additional physical stress on my body. I didn't even know how I could possibly tell anyone about the pregnancy, but I knew I had to.

What kind of sick and cruel joke was this? Welcoming the pope one week and scheduling an abortion for the next. Tossing and turning that night, I fell asleep around midnight, hoping I'd wake up and realize that I was in one of those dreams that was so emotional that it'd only felt real.

But it wasn't a dream at all.

Three days until the pope's visit. I sprang up the next morning focused on work as a distraction. The countdown was on, and Sunday started our daily meetings and briefings. The social office didn't usually work on the weekends, unless there was a large event to prepare for or an event taking place. Thankfully, these were conference calls before the days of Zoom meetings. It saved me from having to make up a lie about why my face was puffy and why my eyes were a deep shade of pink. It saved me from breaking down in front of a team who had no choice but to put their trust in me to execute a flawless week of diplomatic fanfare.

After powering through the ninety-minute call from my bed, I reached out to the White House Medical Unit. They were tasked with the medical care of the First Family, but their services also extended to staff who felt sick or had mild medical issues. The medical unit had offices in the executive mansion of the White House as well as in the adjacent office building. I had gotten to know them pretty well. When I worked on the advance team and traveled around the world, the medical unit assisted with necessary shots and vaccines. I'd also visited a couple of times for cold symptoms, migraines, and basic ailments. Most important, I knew they would keep my secret a secret, bound by a medical code of ethics.

The unit was run by top physicians, nurses, and staff from the US military. The best of the best. With everything happening around the White House that week, I felt secure knowing that the medical team was at least aware of my situation and could react if I fell ill in the midst of the pomp and circumstance of events. Dr. Ronny Jackson, the Obama family physician who later became a Trump-loving Texas congressman, led the office, and he instructed me to come in on Monday morning.

The rest of Sunday was spent on the couch editing briefing memos and timelines, which helped keep my mind off the pregnancy. I also left a message for my gynecologist's office for an appointment as soon as possible. Going to the doctor would help guide me in my options for what kind of abortion I could have, when I could have it, and where I would have it.

By the time the next morning rolled around and the nurse at the medical unit told me, "Your test shows a positive result for pregnancy," I just wanted to get out of there as soon as possible before I broke down crying. I didn't want someone to see me upset and translate that to mean I was breaking under the pressure of the pope's visit. I left the medical unit and snuck through to the back hallway of the White House to an outside pathway behind the floral shop to call my ob-gyn again at the nurse's suggestion.

I wasn't one to go about flexing my status as the White House social secretary around town, but I needed to get in to the doctor that day or the next, Tuesday morning, before the pope's arrival on Wednesday. My fear over not going to the doctor was that something might be wrong inside of me, causing serious complications that week while I was working. I *could not* afford any more complications that week. I told my ob-gyn's scheduling assistant everything—that I was in charge of the pope's visit at the White House, had two positive pregnancy tests via urine samples, hadn't been feeling well, and had been pregnant before. I didn't allude on the phone as to whether I was keeping the baby or not, even though I knew I wasn't.

I had hypertension and was pre-diabetic, so if there was any week for my body to betray me and have a stroke under stress, it would be this one. I wasn't clear enough then on how imposter syndrome affects your physical health. Later in my tenure at the White House, I was rushed to the hospital for hypertension. There isn't a doubt in my mind that my health issues were linked to genetics but also a result of twisting myself inside out to feel comfortable in and worthy of the environment I was in. The constant state of hustle and validation was wearing on my body from the inside out. I felt vulnerable talking to the scheduling assistant about who I was, and to hear myself out loud stress the importance of my job. The doctor's office squeezed me in for later that day.

I was on edge leaving work that afternoon to go to the doctor. I decided to tell a few people in the social office, so they could cover for me if anything came up. Just saying I didn't feel good wouldn't warrant me being out of the office for up to two hours, so I told them the truth. First, my deputy; second, my assistant; and third, two of the associates. My news was met with immediate support. One of the associates, who was one of the bright-eyed interns that greeted me on the first day of my White House employment in 2010, said, "Don't worry, we got you. Whatever you need." I was careful on who I told from there on out, afraid that it would become gossip that would turn into judgment. That was truly the last thing I needed.

My BlackBerry was an extension of me; it was a body part that I checked every three minutes. I assured the team I'd still be checking in. The social office could handle anything without me, but I was still worried about not being there. I was more worried if other people looked for me and questioned why I was gone. But I had to go.

The twenty-minute walk to the doctor's office gave me lots of time to ruminate about my situation. I knew I wasn't going to keep the baby, so my emotions around the actual pregnancy itself were easy to compartmentalize. Although we were pretty good friends, I didn't have a steady relationship with the other person involved, and the idea of having children had fallen away from my mind in my twenties because I just didn't have the time, energy, or finances for it. I didn't have an interest in being a parent. There was no sadness or regret involved in that revelation.

I arrived on the infamous K Street in downtown DC for my appointment. The waiting room was full of women, some with visible bellies and some without. I was ushered back within a few short minutes. With my voice on low volume, I thanked the nurse and reminded her, with an apology, that I needed to rush out of there, reiterating the intensity of the responsibilities I had to go back to in a short ninety minutes. I wasn't trying to sound like I was more important than any other person in that office by again mentioning my credentials, but I just needed to get out of there and back to the White House duties of national security importance—that much was true.

"I'm so sorry. I know y'all are busy but I really need to get back to work as soon as possible," I whispered. The nurse cracked a very irritated smile before looking at the papers in her hand and saying, "We'll do the best we can, but the doctor is running behind."

"Does she want tickets to come see the pope at the White House? Will that work? Do you all want tickets?" I was only half joking, but instead of answering, she started chuckling. We laughed together. The first laugh I'd had in two days, and it felt good. Truthfully, I was humiliated that I'd even joked about that, but the collective laughter offered a balm and calmed a moment fraught with stress.

After the blood was drawn in the lab, I was moved to an exam room to wait for the doctor. What seemed like an hour, but was really twenty-five minutes, went by before the doctor and nurse came into the room to confirm that I was pregnant. I was tired and emotionless. After a slew of questions, I was moved to another room for an ultrasound. This room was chilling—photos of babies on the wall, advertisements for care, formula, classes, and milestones about what to expect in a pregnancy. I was just ready to get this visit over with. The ultrasound showed that I was six to seven weeks pregnant. You could see a very tiny oval-esque shape on the monitor, which was printed out and given to me. When they left the room and I got dressed, my eyes welled up with tears prompted by a flood of self-judgment. I'd let myself get here once again. It was no mystery how I'd gotten here. We all know how. But I was angry at myself for allowing it.

I met the doctor in his office, and he asked me about next steps. I responded quickly that I planned on having an abortion. There was no hesitation, no doubt, and no negotiations within my conscience. The gray-and-white ultrasound didn't make me change my mind. The doctor was very encouraging and said, "You will decide what is best for you," before telling me to schedule a follow-up appointment.

Those simple words provided the permission I felt I needed. That isn't exactly what he said, but that is exactly what I heard. It served as a comfort and reminder that it was my choice and all would be well.

Upon checkout, the medical assistant handed me a folder of expecting-mother information, which I actually wanted to give back to her and say, *I'm good*, but instead I shoved the ultrasound photos in it, put it in my bag, paid my $25 copay, and headed back to the office. I planned on finding a shredder and getting rid of it all. (There were no easy-access shredders at work because we were supposed to preserve all work documents as property of the US government, even Post-it notes.) I didn't need the pamphlets or want them, except the ultrasound. I kept it to show the man involved. I'm unsure why but perhaps it was in preparation for having to prove to him that this was really happening.

I got back to work, threw the folder in my desk drawer, grabbed my binder of event details, and went to our scheduled planning meeting. Jumping right back into work mode, I let it go from there and went about my day, emotionless—only sharing the pregnancy confirmation with those on the social team that I'd informed earlier.

Tuesday, September 22, was twenty-four hours out from the pope's arrival. This was our final prep day— time for me to oversee a full dress rehearsal, from the car arrival on the South Portico of the mansion, to testing of the sound system, checking the lineup of delegates and diplomats, rehearsing crowd entry, reviewing boundaries and exits, choir practice, photography placings, setting of press and dignitary risers, podiums, and chairs—and going through the details minute by minute. Besides the occasional nausea and constant running to the bathroom. Everything in me was focused on these next hours, these next moments that could define my career. If this fell apart or a major detail was missed, it would reflect poorly on the Obamas. That *New York Times* headline would be justified, and I would be dismissed. I cared about my reputation but cared more about the reputation of the president, First Lady, and White House overall.

I lay down to sleep in my office around midnight after taking one last glance at the people lining up outside, hearing their excitement dying down in the night air as they, too, went to bed.

By 6:00 a.m., the White House was already abuzz. I dressed and walked out to the site of the ceremony, the South Lawn. Despite the crowds building near the North Gate of the mansion, the only noise I could hear on the lawn was the vacuuming of the stage carpet, a stapler putting the bunting in place, the swishing sounds of towels wiping the dew off folding chairs, and conversations between colleagues working on last-minute logistics. I couldn't just stand there and watch everyone working. I needed something to do with my nervous energy, so I grabbed a towel from a groundskeeper to help with wiping the chairs.

The long-sleeved, tea-length dress I'd chosen for the event was way snug. When I'd bought it from a thrift store in New Jersey a month prior, it showed no curves of my figure and wasn't so tight. It was the first time I made the newbie mistake of not having a backup dress, but it definitely wouldn't be my last time. This dress *had* to work; it perfectly fit the decorum guidelines for meeting the pope...but then it didn't. As I reached over to wipe the back of a chair, I heard an audible rip and felt a small breeze in my right armpit. Ahhhh! Three hours until the event started, and I had a hole in my dress! I'd already planned on putting paper towels in my armpits to control sweat, but now I also had a hole?!

I went back inside and took the winding marble stairs to the State Floor where the usher's office was.

This small but mighty team was the central location to the residence element of the White House, the living quarters, kitchen, housekeeping, and everything else. I told them about the hole and asked for a sewing kit, planning on taking the dress off, sewing it, and putting it back on. They directed me to the housekeepers two levels down. The clock was ticking, and I took the elevator to the basement level. Everyone was very surprised to see me down there. This area was for the residence workers. White House staff didn't go down there much. The usher's office had called down to the housekeepers and told them I was on my way and what I needed. I raised my arm as they sewed up the hole with me still in the dress, and back upstairs I ran.

The next two hours went by like someone pressed fast-forward on a movie. The crowd of twelve thousand outside flooded into the South Lawn. Everything and everyone was on time. The sun was shining and the weather was sweet. The pope arrived with a smiling entourage as the president and First Lady welcomed him to the United States and to the White House.

I'd chosen a Black gospel choir from DC's St. Augustine Church to sing "Total Praise" by Richard Smallwood. This choice was particularly special to me as I grew up hearing "Total Praise" around my grandparents' house and at church (this was also sung at my 2022 wedding). I knew Black people everywhere would recognize the song on the White House lawn. This particular moment got me a little emotional for many reasons, but mainly because giving this performing opportunity to a Black choir from all choirs around the world and having them sing a song known to my community was everything. I thought: *This, this is the reason why I am here.* I looked over at the stage to see the president and pope swaying in their chairs to the sweet repeats of choral amens.

The leaders exited from outside using the grand South Portico staircase, which led to the Blue Room, where the US protocol office arranged the customary gift exchange. This room was also the backdrop for the photo line. The senior officials of the administration were selected to meet Pope Francis and get a picture with him, the president, and the First Lady. The pope was also excited to get a quick hello from the first dogs, Sunny and Bo. Once that was finished, the pope and President Obama would walk to the Oval Office for a meeting, which the West Wing team and US protocol office led. I secretly couldn't wait for that moment because my part would be finished and I could then turn my focus to state dinner festivities the following day.

Unplanned, President Obama called me over to the corner of the Blue Room where he, the First Lady, Pope Francis, and the Vatican staff were talking. I figured someone needed either water or the bathroom. The president's face didn't read of panic, so I didn't think anything was terribly wrong. I walked over with my binder and BlackBerry just in case he asked something that I had to look up, like the remaining schedule. Instead, the president leaned over to the pope and said, "This is Deesha, our social secretary. She was in charge of making this all happen today."

When I realized that I was meeting the pope, I handed my phone and binder quickly to a colleague right behind me so I could shake his hand. There were no plans in the itinerary for me to greet him. My role was behind the scenes, visible enough to make sure everything was going according to plan, but invisible enough to not look like I was vying to be seen. Although I was part of the White House senior staff, I never felt like it. I was uncomfortable with that power, which spoke to my imposter mentality. I was afraid of being an inconvenience, something that had been rooted in me since I was little.

I was taught to be humble. As my grandfather used to tell me, "God doesn't reward braggers and boasters." I never wanted to be high on my horse, afraid someone would knock me off while telling me I didn't deserve to be up there, so I shied away from being in charge and wanting the spotlight. I wanted to be seen as just another worker, which became messy because it made me a micromanager. We all deserve to bask in our glow of success without inserting a caveat of why or how it happened, trying to downplay it. You deserve to love you and give yourself credit, but it can feel strange if you're not used to it. You don't want to look conceited, stuck up, or better than anyone else—so you just keep it chill and try to fly under the radar.

The pope gestured his hands in a semicircle toward the window before grabbing my right hand in a gentle handshake saying, "Thank you." He kept hold of my hand while the president explained to him what my role was. While the translator communicated every-thing to the pope, I could feel a big smile on my face. I also felt paranoid that I'd extend my arm too far and the black thread holding my dress together would rip!

The five-second handshake seemed more like five minutes. My thoughts drifted off to my childhood in Philly when my brother and I would go to church with Pop Pop, and he would tell me that I needed to confess all my sins in order to go to heaven. I'd cry and say out loud to God how I'd taken twenty-five pieces of candy at the penny-candy store, instead of ten for a dime, or tell Pop Pop that I put on lotion after my bath, but really only did my hands and face. The pastor would put his arm on my shoulder with a half smile and say, "God for-gives you, my dear." My grandfather would recount this story all the time as I got older, and we'd have a good chuckle.

Up until this impromptu moment with the pope, I'd mastered the ability of keeping all my emotions out of the room, solely focused on my work—but now they had arrived, and the pope's grip, smile, and gaze on me communicated that it was okay, God forgives, and he will extend that grace to me. This feeling was over-whelming and confusing. I have never viewed abortion as a sin, but perhaps this powerful religious being right in front of me conjured up my own feelings of guilt. There was no shame in having the abortion, but instead I felt shame for being in the situation where I had to make this choice, again.

When my introduction to the pope was over, I went

scurrying back to the other side of the Blue Room, taking back my binder and phone along with me. The First Lady departed the Blue Room while the president and pope walked through the West Colonnade to the Oval Office for their meeting. Once they were out of eye- and earshot, I joyfully exclaimed, "We did it!"

I would keep a watch over the meeting and the pope's departure to see if I could assist or if last-minute issues popped up, but my colleagues from the State Department and the Oval Office had it handled. I was done, for now.

The months and months of extensive planning had paid off. Everything went according to plan, and we had no noticeable mishaps. I'd led this event to success. It felt so good to finish the papal visit. I knew we had six more adventurous days to go, but in those moments, I'd proved something to myself. I was worthy of this job, and I was deserving.

I stayed in that burgundy dress until the pope departed, then quickly changed into a less fancy dress. It was above the knee and my arms were out, which is why it wasn't an option when rip-gate happened that morning.

God definitely spared me pain and sickness during the pope's visit, but boy did it hit that afternoon. I felt faint a few times and my heart was racing more than normal. I cringed and winced through it, popping into the medical unit to check my vitals just to be sure. There were about thirty-two hours until the small private dinner with President Obama and President Xi was going to take place at Blair House. Across the street from the White House, Blair House is the residence for visiting heads of state and dignitaries. Our office assisted with this dinner, as well as the larger arrival ceremony and state dinner that would also take place for President Xi that week.

I had a finite window to focus on my upcoming medical procedure. For a few hours, it was the biggest thing on my mind. I had to get an appointment the following week when I returned from New York. I hated that I had to put it off for another week, but knew that I needed to buffer in several days to recuperate and one thing that I didn't have that week was time. It was Wednesday. The private dinner was Thursday, state arrival and dinner on Friday, train to New York on Saturday for UNGA festivities Monday and Tuesday, then home on Wednesday. I decided to schedule the procedure for the following Thursday, October 1.

I had a list of providers in Virginia and Maryland that I would call for availability. I was very familiar with Planned Parenthood, which was right in DC, but was afraid someone would see me going in there. I shut my office door and used my personal phone to call around. I found a provider about forty-five minutes away in Virginia and made an appointment for a medical abortion, which I'd never done before, but the thought of not going through a surgical procedure and being able to be home appealed to me.

I was hopeful that maybe I wouldn't need to go through with the medical abortion because all the stress, pressure, and being on my feet the next few days would cause a miscarriage. Not that all miscarriages are the same, but I'd experienced one before that was just like a heavy period. This thought was a relief, not a reality. Again, I didn't care about my health at all. My priority wasn't my well-being. I was solely focused on the job I had to do and staying healthy enough to not be rushed to the hospital in the middle of a busy time. I could imagine people saying, *Well, you know X wouldn't have let herself get into a situation like this as social secretary.*

After confirming my appointments and that my friend Meki agreed to go with me and front the money until I got paid, I requested two days off to recover, and reverted to the work Deesha who needed to prepare for the next day's dinner. I stayed planted firmly in that mode for the next five days as I executed my first state dinner and UNGA receptions perfectly. The biggest hiccup again came with a wardrobe issue as I was heavily advised to find a new dress for the state dinner at the last minute because some folks thought the one I had on (a beautiful African print dress made by a local auntie who sold dresses in Eastern Market) was not appropriate. In all fairness, the person saw me leaving the bathroom without my shawl, so it looked a bit much at first glance. "Do you have any other dresses here?" I was asked two hours before the doors opened for guests. I just wanted to cry but had no time before calling Macy's and asking them to pull dresses for me. I was lucky to have a dope saleswoman on the other end.

I told her who I was, what I needed it for, and that time was of the essence.

"What color, size, price range, style?" she asked.

"Black, 14, under $200, formal, long with sleeves," I responded on speakerphone as I started to leave work to head to the store. I wore a size 12, but needed to go up a little due to my "bloating" situation. I was still in my colorful dress, and the professional makeup I got done was smeared down my face with sweat and actual tears that started to roll down. I was just so overwhelmed and frustrated. *Why does this have to be so hard? Why is everything so hard right now at this moment? It feels like the world is caving in on me and there is no air, no light, nothing.* I started to wonder if people were purposely wanting me to crumble. *Was that the purpose all along, universe?*

I bolted to the third floor of Macy's and tried on a Ralph Lauren dress that was black, long, and sleeveless. It had gold accents and was snug and too long but I knew that with a black scarf, it would be totally fine. It was $250, which I couldn't afford. Lucky me, the tag was at the back of the neck, so I could keep it on and take it back for a refund the following week. Shoes. I had no shoes to match, so the saleslady called down to the first floor and had them pull size 9.5 shoes for me in black. By the time I got down there, there was someone pulling shoes. Tried on one, two, three, and the fourth time was a charm. I grabbed the box and got back to the White House thirty minutes before the doors opened. I paired the dress with the shawl I had. My hair was a mess, face was a mess, and here I was—my first-ever state dinner with an uninvited guest.

Thankfully, even with all this drama, the dinner went perfectly.

As we were winding down the night, the president and First Lady were wishing their honorable guests farewell from the Diplomatic Room on the lower level of the White House. I was standing off to the side in my ill-fitting dress, puffing up the material around the waist to give it some extra room, exhausted but still full of excitement and such a sense of accomplishment. President and Mrs. Obama came back inside and praised me for doing such an exceptional job with the pope's visit and the China state dinner. The president put his hand on my shoulder and said, "That was tough. You and the team did an excellent job," while Mrs. Obama agreed and pulled me in for a hug. I felt my body collapse in that hug, signaling the return of my overwhelming emotions.

If they only knew.

The following Thursday, I went to work for a few hours before heading to Virginia to begin the medical abortion procedure. I took the rest of the day and Friday off, with a plan to return to work on the following Monday. I knew that I needed that time to recuperate—to physically recompose and gather myself so that no one who didn't already know about the pregnancy would ever find out, especially at work. So I swallowed my urge to go back into the office early and took the reprimand. Those days were all I gave myself to terminate

the pregnancy, rest, and recuperate after such a strenu-
ous week. *Three and a half days.*

My pregnancy happened five years into my White
House career and when the political and social world
had its eyes on me. I went back to work while my body
was still bleeding, while I was still in pain and a mental fog. But since I already had an underlying feeling
that people thought I wasn't qualified, I refused to give
them the satisfaction of being right, so I did everything,
including sacrificing my health, to prove my worthiness. I went back to work wearing large dresses to not
constrict my abdominal area. I was more scared to take
off work than I was to do the procedure.

The social office and the medical unit were the only
ones that knew I had an abortion, but I decided to eventually disclose it to others, so they could understand
why I took two days off during such a busy time and
was sometimes absent for an hour or two. It never
occurred to me to disclose this to the First Lady at this
time. I felt it too personal, and although I have no doubt
that it would have been met with support and those
hugs she's known for, I didn't feel it was appropriate.
I never let my pregnancy or abortion affect the profes-
sionalism with which I did my job, or the excellence or
the standard I held myself to. My news was met with
empathy, but by that point, everything in me was so
tired and broken down that I didn't care how it was
received. Widening the circle of who knew I experienced
an abortion brought out my *fuck the world* energy to the
point of tears. I was enraged that as successful human

beings there is an expectation that we push through sickness to prove our productivity, to not be weak, to stay in good standing professionally. I started to question if I modeled and expected this unhealthy practice out of my staff, too, or my past interns. I dropped some of my imposter pounds that week, and realized that I'd been doing this all wrong.

I had to reevaluate who I was trying to prove myself to and why. I was trying to reach an unattainable standard for others. This wasn't a new phenomenon that came with being in the White House for me; it was always there. When the stakes got higher and more profound, this feeling grew to become a full-blown monster that spoke doubt so loudly, I couldn't hear my own voice or the voices of others saying that it wasn't true.

Imposter syndrome likes to grow its roots in situations that are heavily dependent on your ability to show up. I learned to cope and manage by obsessing over details, ruminating over logistics, and making sure every step was accounted for and planned out. I had a saying—*let my work prevail where my confidence fails*, meaning my work was on point, even if the confidence in myself wasn't quite there. This caused me to put work above my health, and, even worse, to expect that from others.

This is why it's so important to address and get a grip on any fraudulent feelings that have made a home within you honestly and holistically. One thing that is guaranteed is that as you grow, you will be faced with new situations and environments that trigger feelings of inferiority. If this goes unchecked, the roots of doubt will grow into trees that grow branches that take over multiple sectors of your life.

Continuing to chip away at this feeling will allow you to eventually detach from an identity that was negatively defined by imposter syndrome. As you do this work, you can denounce and divest from those feelings to truly believe that you belong right where you are, unapologetically. You are required to be accountable to yourself, tuning out the imaginary scenarios and hypothetical questions that get you spun up. You don't benefit from feeling or making yourself small—in your mind or in the world.

Discovering my pregnancy during the biggest weeks of my career wasn't ideal, but it opened my eyes to how self-scrutiny, guilt, and shame twisted themselves into me. It made me think that the outside perception of me, my job, and my reputation were more important than caring for and loving myself. This experience forever changed me. I learned that I am worth more than I ever gave myself credit for. I learned to have compassion for myself for living through past lives and experiences that gave way to negative feelings. I learned that opportunities come and go, as do careers and relationships, so sacrificing myself and my welfare for these things isn't worth it.

This was my wake-up call, and I'm so thankful I answered.

CHAPTER 8

The Debt You Don't Owe

Inauguration day, January 20, 2017, was my last day at the White House and final White House event. The majority of the social office had already rolled off from their jobs, as did other appointees who'd come to the White House under President Obama, a normal practice as presidential administrations come to an end. I think we were all ready. I know that I was. I did all I could do and was proud of so many moments, including watching a group of Black folks swag-surf at the film and music panel festival, South x South Lawn, that we executed on White House grounds, seeing the glow of camping tents lit up at night with Girl Scout troops inside ready to sleep outdoors (we later had to move them into the Eisenhower building as a thunderstorm came down hard—imagine twenty or so girls running with their belongings in trash bags into the White

House!), and witnessing everyday Americans marvel with sheer excitement at seeing President Obama, the First Lady, and let's not forget their dogs, Bo and Sunny.

And on the high end of the dope meter were the last two parties we threw at the White House. One was in collaboration with BET called Love and Happiness: An Obama Celebration that was taped before the election of 2016, but aired after the election. It was the concert of my dreams with BET, De La Soul, Janelle Monáe, the Roots, Jill Scott, Usher, and Yolanda Adams—who sang the house down, even causing a pause in the show as we had to fix the stage after her heel stomped it so hard while belting out the song "Glory" with Common. We repurposed the Italy state dinner tent for the concert and invited as many people as we could. I'd say this is one of the few times I lost all rhyme and reason as I was singing along to "Poison" and "You Got Me." I forgot I was working and got caught dancing by the stage several times. Then there was the after-party with DJ D-Nice, before he was known for Club Quarantine. The party was so lit, and still talked about until this day. With every song played, I wanted to get on the dance floor, but I kept my composure, most of the time. I also didn't find it appropriate to take many photos during my social office years, but I cared a little less toward the end and busted my phone out to take a photo of me with Questlove, Black Thought, and Bradley Cooper. It was my Philly-all-day photo that actually came out blurry because I was rushing and so scared I'd get in trouble. The BET event won an NAACP Image Award, which was lovely, but the memory of that night will forever be one for the books. A cultural and curated toast to an iconic family that I had the honor of serving.

After the election of 2016, it all felt over, although we still had work to do. We had events daily until it was time to officially leave. I always had a visual in my mind that we'd be kicked out the front door like Jazzy Jeff on *Fresh Prince of Bel-Air.* That kept me laughing because the day itself was anything but funny.

On that particularly chilly inauguration day, I oversaw the events that would signify the change of power from President Obama to President-elect Trump. It is a big to-do, all day, with events starting in the morning and proceeding into the evening. My portion would, thankfully, end around 11:00 a.m. Donald Trump would be sworn in that afternoon on the Capitol balcony, making him the forty-fifth president of the United States. The 2016 campaign cycle was brutal, and Trump winning the election was shocking to just about everyone, including him. This would be my second encounter with the Trumps as, per customary tradition, the president-elect and spouse visit the White House the week of the actual election. They came on November 8, 2016, and, despite us also hosting a celebratory event—for the Cleveland Cavaliers, who'd won the NBA title—the day felt like we were going to a funeral. I wore a black dress to mark the occasion. It was…unpleasant. I was so happy that protocol dictated that my job would end as soon as the leaders loaded the car for the US Capitol.

For the second time in my White House career, I spent the night in my office. This time I was thankful that a few colleagues from the military office were doing the same and loaned me an extra cot that lifted two feet off the ground. I brought a quilted blanket from my high school alma mater, a thin tan sheet, and a worn-out pillow from home that I planned on throwing out the next day.

Inaugurations tend to draw crowds into the thousands and, honestly, I didn't want to mix with the crowd of Trump supporters or Trump protestors in the morning commute. I wasn't sure what the scene around the White House would be that night or morning. I had to be up and ready by 8:00 a.m., and with this being my last event, I wanted everything to go perfectly. I also knew I'd be working late the night before, packing and closing up my office, saying goodbye, and going through the long checkout list. I had never been laid off from a job before, but that's essentially what this was. A layoff we all knew about the day we were hired. I'd played this scenario in my head dozens of times, often being left with sobering and detached emotions. Toward the end of the administration, we had two to three events daily, squeezing out every last drop we could making memories in a place this administration would never occupy again. I compare my exhaustion in those last days to someone who is finishing a marathon. During the final miles of the race, you feel strong and accomplished but also a little delirious, just waiting to cross the finish line so you can rest. I wanted to use this last mile on inauguration day to show President and Mrs. Obama that I truly did give it my all, did my best, and they could feel proud knowing they'd chosen me as their final social secretary.

This was my chance to show my gratitude.

Since there were several of us sleeping in the East Wing that night, I made sure to set my alarm nice and early for 6:00 a.m. to get a shower in the ladies' bathroom. I prepped my shower caddy the night before and had my pink flowered ASOS dress hung up and ready to wear. My pearl earrings were in the toe of my heels so I could easily find them and my flats were next to those, because I only changed into heels when it was time to start an event. I hurried through the shower, got dressed, and packed up the bed, my pajamas and toiletries in a small roller suitcase. At this point, I had taken home all of my personal belongings from the office and only had a copy of the last presidential briefing book and schedule, a picture of my nieces and nephew, the day's run of show, and a work notebook on my desk. I had to turn in everything but the picture. White House documents are considered property of the US government and it's illegal to take them home. Unlike some people, we abided by those rules.

My staff on that last day consisted of two people— one who was technically not a political appointee, which means a person/role that stays through various presidential administrations, and my deputy, who was already rolled off but came back to help. She was a longtime Obama devotee, going as far back as the first campaign. It felt only right for her to be there on the president's final day in office. We huddled, hugged, took some pictures, and then got straight to work.

One last time, I called in my breakfast to the Navy Mess. They were such angels, dealing with hungry staff like me who demanded avocado toast, hard-boiled eggs, oatmeal, and tea in the morning, followed by grilled cheese and fries at lunch, capped off with chicken fingers and salad for dinner. These wonderful men and women got to know me well as I often ate every meal at the White House those last several years.

I took my time getting to the West Wing that morning. Walking through those rooms and halls felt a little different. This would be the last time I'd be able to walk freely around the White House with my privileged blue badge. For so much happening that day, the mansion was quiet and hollow. The majority of workers were gone and the residence staff was busy preparing for the changeover of families, so there wasn't much noise. I breezed down the East Wing stairs and took my time walking through all the lower-level spaces, including the East Reception, Booksellers, Map, Diplomatic, and China Rooms, where the presidential china collection is displayed. I took photos down the long hallways one last time: East Colonnade and Lower Cross; I held the rail on the Grand Staircase as I made my way to the State Floor to check out the event rooms and say goodbye to the amazing residence staff, including the ushers, chefs, and butlers.

We'd have another three hours together but I knew this was my last moment to properly hug them and express my gratitude for the love they'd always shown me. The residence staff took it upon themselves to also care for me while I was the social secretary and kept my spirits up with laughs and belly full with food—like the extra plates the kitchen would prepare for me and other staff, despite them being so busy serving guests. They are the backbone of the White House. Never seeking praise or recognition. This moment was the peak of my emotions all day. I had to keep wiping my eyes, knowing that I wouldn't have these talented colleagues with me again. In so many ways, the residence staff reminded me of normalcy. They reminded me of my village back home in the way that they saw me as a person aside from an intimidating job title. We'd talk about outside interests, life, and family. In addition to fixing my vintage clothes on occasion, like during the pope's visit, I'd get updates and see pictures of their kids as they grew up. The majority of them were hardworking and humble, pledging their allegiance to the office of the president, not the individual who held the office. As I walked away from them and wiped my eyes, I quickly grabbed my oatmeal and coffee drink from the Navy Mess while saying goodbye to the sailors as well.

Back in my office, I reviewed the first movements of the day:

DEESHA DYER

7:30AM   SOCIAL OFFICE STAFF, PRESIDENTIAL INAUGURAL COMMITTEE STAFF IN PLACE

9:00AM   POTUS MOVES OVER TO THE OVAL OFFICE

Vice President Biden and Dr. Biden arrive West Executive and proceed to the Blue Room

Joint Congressional on Inaugural Ceremonies and Hill leadership arrive at South Portico and are escorted to the Grand Foyer.

Coffee, water, tea, juices and pastries served in the Blue Room. Mix and Mingle begins

Ushers have someone on hand for coat check

9:15AM   POTUS MOVEMENT FROM OVAL OFFICE TO RESIDENCE

Open-line call with traveling staff from President and Vice-President elect for White House arrival

Upon Deesha Dyer's cue, President and Mrs. Obama proceed to State Dining Room for Flag Presentation

Social Office staff escort the Vice President and Dr. Biden from the Blue Room to Red Room for briefing

9:38AM   VICE PRESIDENT BIDEN AND DR. BIDEN PROCEED TO NORTH PORTICO

Vice President-elect and Mrs. Pence arrive North Portico, greeted by Vice President Biden and Dr. Biden

All proceed to Blue Room for tea. Marine sentries close North Portico doors immediately.

9:40AM   PRESIDENT OBAMA AND MRS. OBAMA PROCEED TO NORTH PORTICO.

President-elect Trump and Mrs. Trump arrive North Portico and are greeted by President Obama and Mrs. Obama. They pose at the top of the portico stairs towards press in this order: Mrs. Trump, Mrs. Obama, President-elect Trump and President Obama.

They proceed through doors to the Blue Room for breakfast.

North Portico doors shut.

I looked at the time and had only a few minutes to be downstairs on the State Floor to welcome Vice President and Dr. Biden. They were part of our first event, the inaugural tea. This customary gathering includes the president, First Lady, vice president, Second Lady, congressional leadership, as well as the president- and First Lady–elect and vice president– and Second Lady–elect. No one ever ate or drank at these things, but it was a chance to crack the awkwardness of the day and have a more intimate chat before being in front of crowds and press. This is the first time all four principals and all four principals-elect would be in the same room.

Vice President and Dr. Biden walked over from the West Wing right before Speaker Nancy Pelosi, Senator Mitch McConnell and his wife, Elaine Chao, who went on to work for the Trump administration, and Senator Chuck Schumer were all set to arrive. There were two staff members greeting and escorting congressional leadership on West Executive Avenue, right outside the West Wing doors, while I was stationed on the State Floor ready to cue the president and First Lady downstairs from their residence to join the tea. I was constantly going back and forth from the radio headset that was connected to my ears and wrist to my BlackBerry getting updates from the Secret Service and Trump advance teams on their timing and arrival. I was also checking news updates on my personal phone to keep abreast of anything spontaneous that the incoming administration would have done. Donald Trump was a natural-born showman who craved attention. It was my job to stay on alert to anything so I could react appropriately if needed and also inform the president and First Lady.

When the president and First Lady arrived at the State Floor, I gathered them with the Bidens and briefed them on the ceremonial arrival. This was one of my most important briefings. Not only was the arrival of the incoming president and vice president going to be on camera, but the press would catch every moment of it up close, as they were stationed right on the North Portico, the front of the White House where the cars pulled up. This was a pivotal moment in the transition of power, a moment that would be plastered all over the media for the next couple of days. The contentious relationship between the principals that had been talked about nonstop added even more pressure to the situation. I just wanted to get the day over with, as it'd be one step toward getting what would be a horrid four years over with under a bully of a president who ignited (but didn't birth) a base of hate. How jarring to watch this transition of power in slow motion.

I talked fast but made sure to not miss any detail: the timing and the cadence of movements; the curated presidential wave to the press cameras, so they could capture the pivotal shot, walking through the doors of the White House to the Blue Room for the event. I was sharp and on point. This was it, my last event. All eight years had come down to this day. I dipped in and out of varying emotions, sometimes in and out of reality. I knew what was happening, I knew this phase of my life was ending, but I just couldn't believe it—*none of it.*

With one eye on my email and the other on the tea, I received notice that the Trump and Pence motorcade was gearing up to leave St. John's Episcopal Church, right across from Lafayette Park in front of the White House. I discreetly whispered to the president and First Lady, vice president and Dr. Biden that it was time to get set for the arrival of the incoming principals. Vice President–elect Pence and Mrs. Pence would arrive first. The Bidens took their place inside in front of the closed doors, awaiting my command to walk outside and stand at the top of the stairs to greet the Pences. It was easier for me to watch out the window than to rely on my email. I spotted the black vehicles pulling up on Pennsylvania, ready to enter the White House grounds through the tall iron gates. I ushered the Obamas to stand off to the side, inside and off camera, where they couldn't be seen, giving them a chance to say a quick hello to the Pences and then make their way to the steps outside to receive the Trumps.

All went according to plan for the Pence arrival. The Bidens proceeded outside and welcomed Mike and Karen Pence to the White House. The Obamas were ever-so-polite and walked over to greet them, as the party of four joined the tea in the Blue Room. The Obamas then got in place in the Grand Foyer, waiting for the wooden doors to be reopened for the arrival of the president-elect and spouse. I quickly briefed the Obamas one last time about what to expect during this transition day, and they went through the doors to take their place at the top of the North Portico steps—the moment the press had been waiting for, the very reason that they were stationed outside. It's a moment that only happens every four or eight years—the "peaceful" transition of power aspect of our Constitution on full display. Except no one knew if this was actually going to *be* peaceful, especially with a crowd gathered that worshiped a man who was inciting and held the face of violence. The level of unpredictability made me afraid for President and Mrs. Obama when they stepped out of the White House doors that day. I'd never really had that feeling before, a general fear for their safety. But everything was different that morning as we were leaving the bubble that we controlled, a bubble in which I felt safe.

I had my head wrapped around a curtain. I found myself gawking at the surroundings, like the press waiting to catch the facial expressions and tension between the two leaders in real time. I observed a line full of cameras and journalists twitching from left to right looking for things and people to cover until the Trumps and Pences actually arrived. Maybe they were hoping to catch a glimpse of the moving vehicles that were arriving out back with the possessions of the new family, or the last few Obama employees roaming the grounds, or perhaps the congressional leaders leaving the tea. The circus had started and the press was hungry to see how it all went down. To me, it still felt like we were living in a weird nightmare. But no, this was reality—my actual reality.

The black limo carrying our guests arrived on time, as expected. President and Mrs. Obama were on hand with all smiles, ready to welcome them to the White House. So far, so good. I'd started to feel a bit of relief. Once we got past this greeting, handshake, and wave, there wasn't much left for them to do except mingle with one another, take a quick break, and then load into the cars for the swearing-in at the Capitol. No problem, super easy—*what could possibly go wrong?* Asking myself this very question was the telltale sign that something was definitely about to go wrong.

As the Trumps proceeded out of the limo, I noticed

Mrs. Trump carrying a very identifiable cyan-blue Tiffany's gift box in her hand. Now, this may not seem like a big deal to most onlookers, but it was a *very big deal* to me because I'd confirmed with the Trump advance team that there *was not* going to be a gift exchange between the couples.

At this point, I'm freaking out. First of all, with practically the whole world watching, we're now accidental brand ambassadors for Tiffany & Co. Second of all, Mrs. Obama specifically asked if any gifts would be exchanged (she did give a gift to Mrs. Bush in 2008 that was tastefully wrapped in an unidentifiable box), and I'd told her, per Trump's advance team, that there wouldn't. Third, what was Mrs. Obama supposed to do with this Tiffany's box—hold it in the photo? It was truly my worst nightmare for my last event. Like, really? With all of this being on camera, I couldn't just walk out and take the box. I saw President Obama take it from the First Lady, and I made a beeline for the door, with an instinct that he was going to try to hand it to someone back inside the house. I was right. My hand met him at the small vestibule and grabbed the box before I shuffled back to the window, put the box down, and escorted everyone through the front doors to the Blue Room.

I was *so mad* over that impromptu gift exchange. So mad. Media was already talking about how awkward it all looked, but I was less worried about the optics and more stressed about the First Lady thinking I hadn't briefed them properly and how could I miss knowing about a gift exchange? There was so much happening that whole day and so many emotions she was feeling, but somehow I'd convinced myself that she was going to be disappointed in *me*. In hindsight, I'm sure that was the last thing on her mind—but I couldn't stop the narrative in my head about how much I'd screwed up this one last event. This was a *chef's kiss* to the end of my White House career. Even though it definitely wasn't my fault, I still wanted to pull the Obamas aside and apologize to them for messing up the arrival. I was afraid I'd made them look silly in front of the press, and that would reflect badly on their last day. I was sick to my stomach with this awful feeling. Even in the chaos and finality of those moments, the Tiffany's box dominated my mind.

But the show had to go on. After twenty to thirty minutes of conversation, the Obamas and Bidens went up to the private residence while the congressional leaders departed for the Capitol. Truthfully, no one seemed to really care about the gift exchange snafu, so I realized I didn't need to, either. The Trumps and Pences were escorted to their respective holding rooms on the ground floor. I briefed everyone separately and told them I'd be back in a few minutes to have them line up to depart. When it was time, I gathered all eight principals back on the State Floor for departure. The discomfort helped distract me from the box incident and my emotions. I lined them up two by two—Dr. Biden and Mrs. Pence were the first to walk out, followed by Vice President Biden and Mr. Pence, then Mrs. Obama and Mrs. Trump, and finally President Obama and Mr. Trump.

I watched them each follow directions from the same window where I'd witnessed the gift exchange, getting into their vehicles and driving away. I felt myself breathe a big sigh of relief that it was over. Not so much the past eight years, but, really, the responsibilities and pressure of the mishaps of that day. This was it and I was completely done; the last duties of my time in the Obama administration were over.

I walked back to my office in the East Wing to grab the last of my things and leave. No more than fifteen minutes after the Obamas had gone, I heard office-remodeling construction and watched as the residence staff started to prepare the private residence for the new occupants, who would move in that afternoon. It felt so over and with all of the Obama administration appointees already gone, I no longer recognized this place.

I turned in my devices and boarded a Sprinter van outside the West Wing full of some West Wing staff who'd closed out the day and shut down the final days of the administration. The mood varied from sadness to disbelief to gratitude as we turned in our equipment and said faint goodbyes. It was both a slow and an abrupt ending to an era. I took a few photos, knowing that as the years went on, the details and memories of our last day would fade. No matter how tired, how relieved, and how anxious I was to be done, I never wanted to forget the feeling of accomplishment, a sense of family that was briefly created.

We did that shit.

We were piled in the van chattering about the day as

we headed for Joint Base Andrews where hundreds of political appointees were on hand to hear from the president one last time and to also wish the family farewell on their journey. It's customary for the outgoing principals to take one last Air Force One plane ride and for the Obama family, that was to California.

They are able to choose a handful of their staffers to go with them, and I was so lucky to be one of them. Also quite surprised, as there was a very long list of supporters, colleagues, and donors who had been with the Obamas since before the first election. I knew the invitation was on purpose and helped confirm that I never needed to feel anything less than amazing—not today, or ever.

I boarded the plane before the Obamas finished saying their goodbyes onstage. I watched out the tiny airplane window as they waved goodbye, walked the red carpet to the plane stairs, and boarded. When they stepped on the plane, we all cheered so loudly, my eyes started to tear up. I had so many conflicting emotions. I was exhausted but also energized, happy it was over but sad that it had all gone by so quickly, emotional and grateful that I'd gotten to be part of this moment in history, but also overwhelmed with why God had chosen me for this journey and why the Obamas had chosen me for these assignments. I'd like to think that they saw in me an outsider who had something special inside to contribute. I think my rough edges and lack of tradition were attractive in that my perspective was fresh and different. They knew that I could learn the protocols and rules, but culture and community were already embedded in me.

Through rounds of champagne and carbs, we laughed and laughed at stories from the past eight years in the White House. Most of the memories started off with "Remember the time..." or "I couldn't believe it when..." Everyone laughed after I recounted the story of me giving my sneakers to Aretha Franklin when her heels were hurting her feet or when Ms. Franklin asked for the heat to be on high, leaving everyone in the East Room sweating as they awaited her performance. She then got on the stage and said it was too hot.

Six hours of recaps later, we landed in California, and it was time to say goodbye. I knew this moment would come and I'd thought hard about what I would say to my bosses in those last moments. I didn't know if I'd ever see them again. I viewed this as my last chance to express what I felt—but I didn't even know what that was. While there were many staffers on the plane who would be continuing in a personal capacity with the Obamas, I wasn't.

I was pretty much a basket case when it was my turn to hug them goodbye. It was around 10:00 p.m. on the West Coast, which would make it after midnight on the East Coast. I had been up for almost twenty-four hours. I was blaming my puffy eyes on that and not the fact that I had been uncontrollably but quietly sobbing. In his larger-than-life voice, the president shouted, "Deesha," as I went in for a hug. I managed to get out, "Thank you for everything," before hugging them both. He touched my shoulder and said, "I hope you know you did a good job," which the First Lady co-signed with "You did."

I watched the First Family walk off the plane in the dark and load up in a black sedan that was waiting for them. They drove off and I scribbled those words of confirmation down on a notepad because I knew that one day I would need to read them again. While President Obama holds significance to me and so many others, the feeling of accomplishment and pride I felt with his simple words had absolutely nothing to do with him or the White House. They were words I struggled to believe about myself. Even the fact that it was the president of the United States saying them didn't automatically put me in a space of acceptance; instead it was as if someone had held a full-length mirror in front of me and challenged me to see myself as brilliant, beautiful, and bold, as much as, if not more than, others do.

I used to think that my inability to see myself through a more polished lens was because of my imposter syndrome. I figured this was a lingering side effect of not thinking I deserved, or had earned, the good things that happened to me. As I was digging up the root of this feeling, going deeper and trying to understand where it all came from, I discovered that I'm guided by a feeling of paying an undefined price to a nonexistent benefactor, for my worth.

After my time in the White House, my therapist asked me something jarring that I didn't have an answer to: "To whom is this debt owed and when is it paid off?" This single question rendered me completely silent for about forty-five seconds, which seems like a whole five minutes on Zoom. Even in therapy, I sometimes try to find a way to keep up with the therapist by saying something clever, joking, or having a comeback. It's partially an attempt to not sound as messed up as I actually feel, to avoid any silent judgment from him or to cause a distraction in the hope of moving on to something else. It goes back to not wanting to confront the hard stuff or be perceived as someone who is so messy. I always want the image of me to seem put together, unexposed. That has nothing to do with imposter syndrome but rather with me not wanting to deal with the feelings that come with other people's judgment.

But this time with my therapist was different. I hadn't thought of this question before, and truthfully it sounded silly. *Obviously, I don't owe anybody shit*, is how I wanted to react, what my inner monologue was pushing me to say, but I quickly remembered that I do pay a hefty price for therapy, so I should be honest. "I don't know. I really don't know," I mumbled instead as I stared at the white wall above my computer screen. Making space for my emotions, he gave me a few minutes before asking, "What is it that you felt right then? What happened?"

While trying to catch my breath in between sobs that seemed to release a little pressure, I replied, "I know this isn't true, but I feel like I owe someone for what has been given to me. Like I made a deal that in order to receive all these things, I must take a lifetime paying back everyone for what has been given to me." I always hated the quote, *Service is the debt we pay for living.* Perhaps because I took it too literally.

Yet if I didn't address this, I would spend a lifetime

being addicted to validation as proof that payment for my worth was accepted. The payment would be me doing good deeds. I then would get validated for this by someone. It was transactional with the payoff being my worthiness. These types of interactions happen without me even knowing. It became a way of living, a blueprint I designed for my relationships and care for myself. As I started to unpack this in therapy, I made the connection that my consistent overwhelm came with people-pleasing in order to be accepted or validated. I wanted to do everything all at once, all the time to help shape the perceptions of me that others would have. If someone saw me working really hard, I would be classified as a hard worker. If I always gave of my time, money, and resources, I'd be seen as generous and compassionate. If I had my hand up for every opportunity, I'd be seen as a go-getter. None of these things are necessarily bad, but it's all I focused on. A cycle of doing things to be perceived as good, as worthy. Paying a debt that I didn't owe to the world.

As I started to put actions into place to reverse these behaviors, I sought out ways to reduce my workload. I needed to decrease the amount of stress from trying to do too much. I hired an assistant and it absolutely backfired because people were used to seeing me juggle a million things. I was called noble and strong for burning myself out. Upon getting some help, I "became" this person who sold out because I needed and asked for help. Even those closest to me made fun of it—like okay, y'all just want to see me stressed out with high blood pressure every day? All of a sudden, I was being perceived as someone who needed help and was dependent and not in the good way. It was infuriating to say the least, but I felt a bit of relief knowing that I was breaking a bad habit that affected my physical health, and also my mental health. I needed help. We all need help. When I cleared away the debris of my imposter syndrome, I tapped into a love of self that was hidden deep beneath the surface. It was living in the shadow of an unhealthy relationship that I formed with myself. One that caused delusions around who I was—which is an impeccable, amazing, smart, creative, fun, and loving human being. That didn't come from my highly visible and powerful job. Those things were curated by me, and now I can see them so clearly. It's the most beautiful thing in the world.

I was committed to not allowing myself to embrace all that I was and all that I am. You may be in the same place. Hell-bent on justifying your existence through the validation of others, people-pleasing, or even your accomplishments. There's a reason why you are put in positions that amplify your greatness, and it's not because you owe anyone anything and not because you got lucky; it's because you are you. It sounds so simple, but it's not really. We make so many excuses for why good things happen to us instead of just accepting, enjoying, and relishing those moments.

You'll never be able to see your light standing in your own shadow. Move and get out the way.

CHAPTER 9

After the Fact...

I was finally out of the White House and I worked heavily on prioritizing and reclaiming the identity of my former self, who I was before I went to Washington, while also embracing who I'd become against the backdrop of all these amazing experiences. That person was full of so much doubt and worry, anxiety and fear, but she also possessed a carefree and artistic spirit that danced until the sun came up, had impromptu brunch dates with friends, and took long walks for hours listening to music. I'd missed that part of me. It got a little lost.

While the world was engulfed in the flames of Donald Trump becoming president, my life was starting to feel reserved and introverted. It took me a while to stop searching for two phones, as I'd gotten used to having one for work (BlackBerry) and one for personal use (iPhone). I was still checking my emails like I did when I was at the White House, paranoid that I'd miss something time-sensitive. I lounged a lot in my bed and on my couch watching movies. For the first time in over sixteen years, I was unemployed. My bank account leveled out at around $8,000, which, to me, was a lot of money to have saved. I didn't worry about paying my bills because I had enough to cover them for at least four months.

When presidential administrations end, it is procedural to go through workshops about filing for unemployment, updating your résumé, networking, and applying for jobs. I was often too busy to take time away from the East Wing to attend those classes, but I was front and center for the unemployment tips, as I knew I'd be utilizing that option and filing as soon as I could. Even though I technically couldn't afford to take time off after the White House, I knew that I had to. I was physically and mentally exhausted, proven by a short hospital stay a month before we ended. Unemployment was the time to catch my breath, rest, and start to wrap my head around the experience I'd just lived. I was in a very privileged position of not having many expenses, so with the money I'd saved, getting paid out for unused vacation, and unemployment, I was able to do absolutely nothing for a few months. I watched as my White House colleagues started senior positions in tech and entertainment in cities like New York, San Francisco, Seattle, and Los Angeles. Some stayed and settled down in DC, continuing their government work in the private sector or on Capitol Hill. But as for me and my tired self, I was chilling.

Like everyone else, I believed that after having a job at the White House on my résumé, an out-of-this-world job would be super easy to obtain. I mean, I was practically at the highest level of the federal government, working for the first-ever Black president and First Lady. I orchestrated dinners with world leaders, concerts with entertainers, and tours with the academic elite; I hosted athletes from around the world. I interacted with embassies both in the US and abroad, invited activists and community leaders to sit at tables of political influence, and carried out my duties with excellence. We got shit done and had fun, a vibe that is hard to balance and perfect under such scrutiny and pressure. And...I had the Obama name behind me. Surely, surely I would find a job, right?!

It couldn't just be any job, either. I wanted something just as prestigious and also something that allowed me to have a life after 7:00 p.m. I didn't want to accept anything below $118K, my beginning and ending salary as social secretary. I was pretty certain that I didn't want to continue doing events, and that was what everyone in Washington, essentially, knew me for. It didn't take long for my quickly dwindling bank account to confirm that I couldn't stay unemployed forever. Actually, I couldn't afford to stay unemployed for another two months.

At the time, I was also planning a move to the Virginia Beach area to be with someone I had no business

dealing with. It was so foolish, and I was simply looking for something, someone, to fill my time and guide
me on my next steps—and moving to an area where I
knew absolutely *no one* seemed like a bright idea at the
time. I had no job, I had little money, and the beach was
calling my name—but so were my bills!

Thankfully, the relationship soured, and the move
never happened. As all that hit the fan in the summer
of 2017, I ended up getting an offer to cover for a friend
who was going out on maternity leave for six months.
She was the chief of staff to Darren Walker, the president of the Ford Foundation in New York City. It came
with a great salary, excellent benefits, vacation days,
and a chance for me to try out NYC.

After growing up in Philly, New York seemed so big
and overwhelming, expensive and impossible—so getting a little taste of that life was scary but also exciting.
Except I ended up moving to Weehawken, New Jersey, instead of New York City itself. I had a friend who
lived in a three-story house that had been converted
into apartments, and the basement unit was open. It
was very inexpensive, and my friend and her family
lived above me, so it offered me a built-in community,
albeit with a kind of hellish commute scarred by traf-
fic, crowded buses, dangerous-ass jitney vans, and lines
upon lines at Port Authority to head back to Jersey. It
wasn't the best situation, but it definitely wasn't the
worst. It allowed me to start a new life and step into the
field of philanthropy.

The thought of this was exhilarating, as I had always

been on the other side of the table, the nonprofit side, begging places like Ford for money for initiatives and programs in the community. In my new role I'd actually work within the hallowed walls of this big and esteemed name. And to do it all under Darren, who is an iconic leader, was like going back to school and getting paid for it. Working at Ford was also a chance to understand how grant giving worked and get up close on the mechanics of its operations. If anything, it'd help me learn about funding for beGirl.world Global Scholars, an organization I co-founded in 2014 that diversifies study abroad by encouraging, empowering, and equipping Black teenage girls to travel the world. My co-founder and friend Marcella and I, both travel lovers ourselves, were startled by the fact that only 6 percent of study-abroad students are Black. We had monthly meetups and activities on the weekends, funded passports, and took girls on both domestic and international trips to places like England, France, and Spain—these trips always occurred during the month of August when the Obamas were on vacation. While we obtained a few grants, mostly everything was funded by donations, and at the expense of myself and Marcella. We needed that big philanthropy money, though!

New York City was a hard jump. I was rebuilding my life after eight years of operating at the highest intensity. By this time, I had already done some deep identity work through therapy—mostly in the realm of not allowing my accomplishments and achievements to define my identity. This was a priority because, in the past, I'd fallen into this trap that took me on a roller coaster of emotions based on whether I was achieving enough, which we all know can come and go. NYC had never been on my radar, never part of a long- or short-term plan, but I vowed to make it a fresh start for me, saturating myself in theater and hip-hop, restaurants and walks in the park.

But once my temporary job at Ford ended in December 2018, I had nowhere else to go, professionally or personally. My six-month lease in the basement unit in Weehawken was up, and I didn't want to stay there. The thought of going back to a Trump-filled DC made me feel ill, plus I wanted to leave that life behind to see what else was out there.

I had taken a short hiatus from dating while I figured myself out. It wasn't that I didn't want to find someone; I just didn't feel in the space to. I had never really dated and needed to learn how. Sure, I'd had relationships, but they were usually formed after going out with someone once or in high school. And sure, I had casual flings, but they usually lasted years and years, getting my feelings all tangled to only end up hurt in the end. I needed some time to figure out what a renewed self meant for a romantic partnership.

During one of the beautiful spring days that New York is known for, a friend and I were dining together in Chelsea when she told me that she knew someone with an open studio apartment in Brooklyn for several months. I quickly jumped on it, was connected, and moved into a hip studio connected to the Barclays

Center in Brooklyn. This was a dream come true for me, a hip-hop lover and journalist who had been to plenty of concerts, festivals, and dance battles in Brooklyn. It was the home of Jay-Z and Biggie. It had the best pizza and Jamaican food. It was a borough full of block parties that captured the soul of the people, Black people. The studio was also a ten-minute walk from one of my favorite spots, Sugarcane, which has the best jerk wings in the world. I had access to several trains and vintage shops galore. After that sublet was up, I found another, also in Brooklyn, this time in Clinton Hill, where I found a church home around the corner and sealed in my Sunday routine of going to church, taking the bus to Dumbo for the Brooklyn flea market, usually leaving with some vintage art, clothing, or décor, having lunch on the water, and then taking the bus home.

I was taking on side event projects here and there, while still running my nonprofit, but had enough money saved up to make unemployment for a few months possible. I leaned deeper into healing work by getting a personal trainer to help regulate my high blood pressure and pre-diabetes. I also started seeing a new therapist who worked extensively with Black women. This was a pivotal point in my life and with imposter syndrome, because it's when I noticed that all my work was paying off. I mean, I had no job and no real place to live, yet oddly enough, I was calm. Unlike times in the past, I wasn't kicking myself for not having it all together and not having it planned out better. I wasn't comparing myself with former White House colleagues who had fancy jobs in finance or tech. I wasn't upset about not continuing my career in Washington. I was by myself, focused on myself. My church centered mental health in its faith teachings, which contributed greatly to the feeling that, despite all that was unsettled in my life, *it was all going to be okay.* I had the testimony. I had the proof. I refer to church, the gym, and therapy as the trifecta of what changed my life, altered my perspective, and helped me get past the healing stage enough to find joy in the stillness and peace in the uncertainty.

I had also built a hustle public speaking about everything from my White House experience to community activism, but the most requested topic from audiences at colleges, corporations, and nonprofits was imposter syndrome. The term had blown up so much that it made its way into every industry, taking on a life of its own. Standing in front of audiences recounting these very stories through laughs and tears was such a release. To know I was making someone feel more whole, more loved, and not alone was the best honorarium that I could ever ask for. Don't get it twisted, though, I also got paid!

Just as I was getting a little anxious about where I'd live after the sublet and how I'd make money, the Ford Foundation called me back to be the permanent chief of staff, after the former COS left for a great opportunity on the West Coast. I gladly accepted, stepping back into the familiar role with familiar people. This kicked off my own personal renaissance, including signing a lease for a beautiful apartment in dreamy Harlem, starting dance classes, and taking a few writing seminars. I finally felt comfortable doing some extracurricular things with this extracurricular money. It'd been over a year since I left my DC place. My belongings were scattered up and down the East Coast—at friends' houses, my dad's, two storage spaces, and also with me. Moving and getting settled in Harlem was messy with my life in boxes for a while as I pieced back together what a home, my home, would look like. It felt fine, actually more than fine. Summers with the window cracked in Harlem, being serenaded by car stereos and loud conversations after the club on the corner of my street let out, became my soundtrack every night, a soundtrack to a newfound life. Well, that and Cardi B's debut album, *Invasion of Privacy*. I played it out to the point where I thought my neighbors would come knocking.

Yeah, it's not a threat, it's a warning.

I ran the song "Be Careful" into the ground. The beat, the lyrics, the IDGAF vibe. I was on it, I felt it.

On my forty-first birthday in January 2019, I hosted a dinner for twenty people at a restaurant in Midtown Manhattan. It was low-key and consisted of family, high school friends, former and current co-workers, and some other folks I'd met in my year in the city. My personal trainer and church counselor also attended, and although I invited my therapist, Dr. J, she quickly schooled me that it would be inappropriate to attend. Oops! I explained that I understood, but she was part of my trifecta, and I wanted her there to celebrate this renewed part of me. As nice as that sounds, it didn't work! For my birthday, I also curated a Harlem-themed photo shoot, which actually happened right in the middle of a massive hair loss (due to blood pressure meds). I covered my hair with hats and cute, vintage scarves so it was okay. I still felt beautiful.

Truth be told, I didn't recognize this person in the mirror. My inner work was still being done but the weight of doubt was lifted enough that I could breathe easier, love easier, and move with a protection of peace around me. Just picturing this time brings a smile to my face and warmth to my heart, but things started to feel a little too right—shall I say boring—in a way that I got used to. I was anchored in a safe space, which was great because that's what we all want, right? Safe spaces, but something didn't feel entirely right.

Once I got a good handle on my imposter syndrome, the healing built a guardrail around my life. It helped keep me protected, but also kept me content in a way that I'd never been before. This feeling of contentment and security scared me. It scared me into trying something risky, just to shake things up a bit. Sometimes, when we're used to chaos and trauma, contentment can be a scary thing; it can make us feel like this good thing could never last too long. I was set up to always be waiting for the other shoe to drop. I wasn't used to stillness. I had to learn to sit with it and learn that boredom was okay. Well, it was better than anxiety. I ran to my journal, where things become more clear as the transition from my heart to hand to paper occurs:

This place is not familiar. You have not been here before.

What you thought is no longer. What you learned is no more.

This place is not familiar. You have not been here before.

There's a chair for you to sit down or walk around. Enjoy the view.

This place is not familiar. You have not been here before.

I have not been here before.

I have not been here before.

This wasn't before. I wasn't a child vying for belonging. I wasn't a teenager loudly rebelling to be heard. I wasn't in my twenties struggling to keep a roof over my head. I was no longer a White House employee who focused on mentally and emotionally paying a debt for my worth. The cracks of my foundation were now cemented and patched up. The scars were visible, but the wounds were healing. *I had not been here before.*

I took a plunge and signed up for the Hinge dating app. This wasn't my first time trying out online dating. At this point, I hadn't tried dating in about a year. In the past, I'd added and deleted dating apps about once a week, mainly when the free trials were up, but the results had been so absolutely terrible that I was hesitant to try again. I didn't have the patience to give it a chance longer than that. My vibe was right and mixing in another human was risky. It might take me off this healing journey. My mindset wasn't fixated on a relationship or marriage, but more on finding a best friend / companion / lover? I really didn't know, but I at least knew I wanted to try. My string of co-dependent relationships and meaningless flings was caused by knowing but not believing that I deserve better. Just like with validation and approval as a substitute for self-confidence, intimate romantic partner relationships became a quick way to feel wanted. I felt more optimistic than ever about dating. The renewed and healed sense of self gave way for me to attract a different kind of life partner—one who was beautifully imperfect, but trying. I went into it with no hopes of meeting the love of my life, just hopes of meeting someone dope that I clicked with and could occasionally make out with.

I was trying to manifest a Black girl *Sex and the City* experience, as much as that makes me cringe now. Megan Thee Stallion's "Hot Girl Summer" had come out and as carefree and lovely as that sounded, I knew my ass couldn't handle a hot girl summer. I wanted a chilled summer. I wanted random dates that might end the morning after. I was also in the best shape of my life physically and, more important, mentally. I felt ready for a healthy partnership in a way I hadn't before. The maturity and clarity that came with being over forty allowed me to be free, but also cautious.

Between the back-and-forth, inappropriate messages, and dud dates (*if this is what dating is like now, maybe it's best I opt the hell out*), I was getting tired of so much attention being spent staring at my phone, refreshing, and looking for new prospects. Every time I opened the app, I'd laugh thinking about how dumb it was, how dumb I was, and how I actually wanted to meet someone in person. I decided to delete it the next day when I woke up. On one of my obsessive swipe-a-thons, as me and my friend Jennifer called them, I noticed a photo of a man on a boat wearing a backward visor hat (*ugh, really? Is this man twenty-five?*). Scrolling through the rest of his photos, I thought he was attractive, and his answers to the mundane questions were corny but entertaining. I swiped right thinking, if anything, *Maybe I'll get to go on that nice boat in the photo.* He also said he was from Connecticut in his profile. Oh, my goodness—*What if he's rich, from Greenwich, and owns a boat?* I was half joking but also envisioning yacht-life photo shoots in the future.

Turns out, me and this boat man, named Wes, swiped on each other! We chatted on the app for two hours before switching to our cell phones. We went on our first date June 11, where I found out that it wasn't his boat, and he wasn't rich! Our first date was chaotic, as I was running late from work and I didn't want to flake on him, so I had him meet me at my job. The food was awful at the restaurant we went to, and he talked a lot. I found out he worked at a nonprofit, had been married before, didn't have or want kids, and was in the Peace Corps in his twenties. He lived in a fourth-floor studio walk-up on the Upper West Side and had a cat named Gus. And as for me, I spent the conversation telling White House stories, so he'd think I was so cool—which he did, but in a time when I was working on defining my identity *outside* of my former job, I didn't mean to ramble on about it. Even still, we laughed all night. And that night, I shared my last first kiss with a man because, five years later, he is now my husband!

The maturity and clarity I'd gained with age and with learning to manage my feelings of unworthiness made me more ready for this moment than I had ever been, allowing our relationship to blossom without me second-guessing myself and feeling that I wasn't worth such a wonderful man or such a calm, content, and fulfilling life.

Life was good and not just due to the budding romance, but because there was an ease within me that was contagious. I felt like I was elevating in so many arenas in my life. My energy was aligned with the universe and everything felt right. It gave me leeway to take risks, and as my job search started to ramp up in 2018, I received a call from the assistant director at the Harvard Kennedy School Institute of Politics. She called as I was exiting the subway on my way to the Hearst Tower offices in Midtown Manhattan to meet about a philanthropy summit that my boss, Darren, was participating in. I'd never felt *so* New York as when I exited that train, changed into my high heels, and took a call at the same time. I had nightmares about the first time I visited the Condé Nast offices after the White House was over. I was on a networking tour, getting advice and trying to explore what was next for me and my career.

I had to get ready in the Penn Station bathroom (before the fancy Moynihan remodel) since my train was late getting to New York from DC, leaving me to scramble and hope that no one in our important meeting could smell that the bathroom was my dressing room. So this time walking into Hearst, I made sure I was sharp, and had gotten ready at home.

As I scurried to find a quiet space ascending from the noisy subway, the assistant director on that call informed me that my name came up from the current fellows and students as someone they'd be interested in having as an Institute of Politics resident fellow. "Who? Me?" I couldn't believe my ears. Harvard? As in the Ivy League university in Cambridge?

The woman on the other end of the call told me they were accepting proposals and to think about it. *Do these people know I only have a community college degree and couldn't even get into a state school, let alone an Ivy League school? And now they want me to come instruct and guide their students?* It was laughable. What?

My imposter syndrome was on hiatus. I didn't doubt I could be a teaching fellow and do a good job—those days were now behind me. It was more the disbelief that I'd found my way onto their radar. Ultimately, I decided not to apply that year. I wanted to stay at Ford. I didn't want to walk away from a job I enjoyed, one that paid well, and one that I was learning so much from. I didn't know what I was missing, so it wasn't that big a deal to me, and Harvard informed me that the door was open for me to apply another time. It felt really good to be considered for such a prestigious fellowship that only selects six fellows each semester.

Thinking about leaving my role at Ford scared me financially, above all, but leaving that job also meant leaving the safety net of flexibility and security I'd created for myself. Still, there was another side that was calling me to explore being back in community or doing something in a more creative field. While Ford had departments that were heavily steeped in both, it was clear that I didn't have the experience or qualifications to dive into either.

I decided to apply for a fall 2019 fellowship. It had been a whole year since my conversation with them, and I knew going in that there would still be tough conversations ahead. Their interest in me in 2018 did not equal an automatic acceptance in 2019. I worked and reworked my proposal, just as I had my application for my original White House internship. Friends and former colleagues proofread it and gave me feedback to make it stronger. I talked to alumni and current students there, asking them to weigh in on it. I'd only been dating Wes for a few weeks at this point, but I made him read it over several times as well. Talk about testing a new relationship!

I handed in a proposal titled *Imposter to Impact*. I prayed that I'd at least get an interview. And I did, first with students at the Harvard Institute of Politics, next with the staff, and last with the executive director. They commented on how real the proposal was, the vulnerability I'd shown in using my own life, the urgent need for students to have a class like this, and the benefits of me being on their campus. I was so nervous during this process, but I knew I'd handed in a good proposal. I knew that if given the chance, this class could change the trajectory of a young person's life and instill in them that they are worthy, beautiful, valued, and deserving. It meant so much that I could tell students this at a young age—that they wouldn't have to wait until their late thirties, like I did, to hear this message. That such a message could save them from heartbreak, depression, and bouts of doubt was exciting to me.

Thankfully, Harvard thought the same, and I left Ford. I moved to Cambridge, Massachusetts, in September 2019, fully focused on the resident fellowship for four months. I mastered a balancing act at Harvard. I was so excited to be there on campus with the students. It was a beautiful rush to walk around the grounds week after week, meeting with the broader college community; however, I also fully recognized that an elite white-centered institution like Harvard wasn't innocent in keeping up the toxic exceptionalism, operating with a stain of systemic racism, sexism, and classism. I refused to get caught up in the respectability politics, instead focusing on the amazing experience with the brilliant students who in their own right were struggling with belonging.

Being selected for the fellowship did more than thicken my already impressive résumé. It allowed me to continue believing that I was capable of more than what I could see in front of me. It reminded me to keep my faith as a high priority and that doing the work on myself to divest, dig, and nurture will harvest everlasting results, even if they are unknown to me.

Being fully submerged in the fellowship was my choice. I prioritized speaking time with the students, getting to know and support them, discovering the campus, attending lectures and other classes, and living the adult version of a life I'd missed out on by dropping out of college when I was seventeen. I was so proud of myself for reaching an Ivy League school with a community college degree. I walked to the Kennedy School on campus from my apartment fifteen minutes away so thankful, so tall. I absolutely loved it so much that I lived in the present and didn't think about what life would be like post-fellowship. My loose plan was to start reaching out in my network for opportunities to find a job in impact or operations work. I was blissfully naive about the job market.

I knew I wanted to be in the corporate social responsibility, social impact sector and was willing to take a pay cut for it, or even step back from leadership roles to take one where I could learn some fundamental things I'd missed on the quick White House rise. I also thought of a long-term plan to get more experience in programmatic and community work and then perhaps go back to the Ford Foundation for a job that aligned with my present interests.

Within several months of great conversations, two offers (that I turned down), and one step away from accepting a position at a job in London, the world was hit with the COVID-19 pandemic. Ever since I'd begun working in government, I had wanted to live overseas, and this job was my chance. Wes and I decided that we'd figure out how to navigate the distance since he worked in New York City. Unfortunately, the position in London was no longer an option as industries and companies halted hiring and started laying off workers. While I was upset, there were people dying by the hundreds all around us. It seemed trivial that I wouldn't be able to live out my international dreams.

I moved into Wes's fourth-floor walk-up studio apartment on the Upper West Side for what I thought would be two weeks while the world got COVID under control enough for life to return to what we called "normal." Up until this point, Wes and I were doing great but had no plans to move in together; we weren't talking about marriage, just enjoying an NYC romance with no pressure. I loved my own space, the sanctuary I created for myself in Harlem.

Thankfully I had a good amount of money saved up, so not actively making income for a few months was okay and it allowed me to volunteer in communities that were hard hit by the pandemic, mainly poor Black and Latino neighborhoods that were already struggling. This quickly spread to friends from companies asking my advice and operations expertise on how to best aid these communities.

I had to take a step back. My involvement in community work had gone back over twenty years, and the majority of it was for free. I volunteered my time, even with large corporations that actually had the capital to pay me. I thought back to the height of my imposter syndrome when I didn't have boundaries to my time or knowledge. A time when I was proud to give everyone access to me. I fell into the trap of being a Black woman who labored for free under the guise of "out of the goodness of my heart."

I was working with a major global financial services firm on getting funds and resources to a poor community. I was up early for meetings, helped set up the infrastructure for giving, sat in on tons of calls, and worked late into the night, for free. I approached them about getting paid and they said, "We don't have money in the budget for that." I was both stunned and disgusted, but realized that if I stuck around, they'd continue to use me. I felt guilty for the community partners that I had to abandon, but I knew and demanded better. Wes and I were sitting on a worn blue futon watching Netflix discussing the ridiculousness of their response.

"I should set up my own company so I can get paid for consulting," I blurted out.

As nonchalant as possible, Wes said, "Sure. Why not?"

I knew nothing about having my own company, nor had I ever wanted to be an entrepreneur, but I knew that I had the talent, contacts, and experience that could benefit companies, as already witnessed by my previous volunteer work with this financial services firm.

"It'll only be until the pandemic is over and people start hiring leadership again," I said. My venture, Hook & Fasten, was born in June 2020 with a roster full of clients. Companies paid me to be a thought partner, idea generator, and bridge to the people and changes that were needed on the ground. I was trusted by both the C-suite and those in the community. Wes also came to work for Hook & Fasten, which looking back is a miracle. We operated a business together in a studio apartment, a year into our relationship—and survived!

A month into launching the business and three months after COVID made its way across the nation, a Black man who was a father and son was murdered by cops in Minneapolis. His name was George Floyd. His murder was captured on video. The world watched all eight minutes and forty-six seconds of his last waking moments on earth. This was on the heels of a Black woman, Breonna Taylor, being murdered by cops in Louisville while she was sleeping and a Black man, Ahmaud Arbery, being murdered by racists when he was jogging in Georgia. I was numb as a coping mechanism. This is not to be confused with becoming desensitized. There was anger on top of anger that built every day when I saw the news. I was not shocked or surprised. I was seven when the MOVE bombing took place in Philadelphia, killing eleven Black people, and thirteen when I watched a Black man, Rodney King, get beaten by cops on live television. Unlike after the deaths of Trayvon Martin, Freddie Gray, Michael Brown, and Sandra Bland, I was out of the White House and no longer felt confined by my government job to not expressing my feelings. But what could I really do?

The world reacted in a way I'd never seen. There were uprisings across the nation. The majority were performative, while others were revolutionary. I was angry at the obvious things, but also angry that it took George Floyd's death to realize the supremacist state in which we all have lived and to which we've all been conditioned. The discussions went beyond the relationship between law enforcement and Black people; questions about how Black people are treated in various sectors began to spring up in the aftermath of the protests and demands. Black Lives Matter once again made it to the mainstream, appearing in storefronts, on clothing, in company mission statements, and in all forms of entertainment. I remember heading to Trader Joe's on the Upper West Side for our biweekly grocery run and seeing an all-white brigade holding signs that said HONK IF YOU BELIEVE BLACK LIVES MATTER. Then walking into the store I saw workers with buttons repeating the same message. It felt weird and cringe. We asked for justice. We really just asked to live, not have this slogan become a trend to make everyone else feel good about themselves and their complacency enforcing a hierarchy that goes back hundreds of years.

Companies wanted in. They wanted to show that they, too, believed that Black Lives Matter, although they didn't have a Black person in leadership, had no measures in place for racial aggressions, and held a company culture that signaled to Black employees everything but that they mattered. I thought about all the bullshit I'd been through in my professional life of internalizing the racism I was exposed to in institutions and corporations. I let them make me believe that I was incompetent, not polished, not qualified, dumb, and undiplomatic. I let them make me feel I carried a bad attitude as part of my core and that my boldness, uniqueness, and fire were problems. This twist of deception, gaslighting, and manipulation was always my base for my activism of working directly with youth to instill in them how outstanding, beautiful, and Black they are—so when the oppressors come knocking, they will resist and not bow down, as I had done so many times.

I sat in quiet rage just writing pages and pages of feelings that I didn't know where to place. In 2012, I drafted an essay that's never been published about how the killing of Trayvon Martin sealed my decision to never have children. The essay is now six pages, as it becomes longer every single time another murder happens.

I didn't have any grand awakening when George Floyd was murdered. But the rest of the world acted like they did. Hook & Fasten's work became more DEI-focused and I was asked to facilitate race conversations, conduct trainings, do diversity audits, and curate meetings that would "educate" people on Black issues. We were asked to start Black book clubs and employee resource groups, advise leaders on language, and work on hiring equity. I built up a strong roster of on-call consultants who focused on race in the workplace to include white supremacy, power structures, aggression, and bias.

While on our first road trip out of New York since COVID began, I received a call from a friend who asked to come in and help facilitate conversations between employees and leadership about being Black in a majority white workspace. I got off the phone with conflicting feelings of excitement about building my client roster but also disgust that this was happening on the back of a Black man's death.

"I'm not sure I can do this," I told Wes one day as we pulled into a rest stop somewhere in New Hampshire. We were returning from Loon Mountain, where we'd stayed in a cabin for four days.

"What do you mean?" he asked. I didn't feel like explaining it to my white boyfriend at the time so I just replied with a simple, "I don't want to talk about it right now." He didn't push, and we got in the car to keep driving.

I listened to the hopeful side of me that was telling me repeatedly how I could make a difference and be able to communicate all the things to leadership that the Black employees don't have the safety net to say. As I signed contracts, one day I received a call from a former White House colleague who asked me if I'd be open to making a statement about George Floyd and the murders of Black people on famed comedian Leslie Jordan's Instagram. I told the friend I'd think about it and text him back. Leslie Jordan, a charismatic gay actor and comedian, built up a million followers on Instagram through his funny and feel-good stories that kept people's spirits up during the pandemic. He was witty, talented, and he spoke with a southern accent. He wasn't known for his political commentary or social justice knowledge and admitted that those things were of interest, as he was heavily involved in the AIDS movement in the 1980s and '90s, but what was happening in the world in the wake of George Floyd's murder was out of his expertise.

My first thought was to help them find someone who is publicly known for speaking out, from some of my friends and peers that I looked up to. I was truthfully scared of not saying the right thing, perhaps feeling like I'd been far enough away from my activist roots to come across as authentic or credible. I analyzed what I would say over and over and didn't like the anxiety. I wanted to truly say, *Fuck everyone. We just want to live and mind our business.* Or say something that could be translated as *an eye for an eye* and look like I was advocating for violence back. Always a Philly girl, ready to fight!

So I texted the friend.

"Thanks for thinking of me, but I have some names of people who I think may be better for this."

"He wants you. Why don't you want to do it?" he texted back.

"I just know some really dope known people who would be more qualified."

"Okay, but he'd rather you do it."

But why? It was explained to me that Leslie didn't want someone who had talking points or was known for speaking out. He wanted perspective from an everyday person who lives with being Black every single day. After some back and forth with Leslie, I agreed to do it.

There were multiple takes but I finally landed on one that was raw emotion, a few stumbles, and a message that leaned heavily on accountability, action, and reckoning not being Black people's cross to bear. I never felt "good" about doing the video, as the conflicting feelings kept rising, but I did feel proud that I didn't disqualify myself from speaking with authority and vulnerability on a sensitive topic. I did the whole imposter syndrome monologue in my head of whether people would think I was fake, performative, or trying to extend my fifteen minutes of fame from the Obama years.

Within days, the video racked up thousands of views and an array of comments that ranged from support for the message to hate and name calling. As a result, Hook & Fasten was flooded with requests from companies who wanted us to help them. Many conversations ended once we realized that companies were interested in revising, not dismantling, power shifting, and rebuilding, their DEI strategies or when I'd ask if the Black employees were getting paid to lead affinity and resource groups. Those two things always let me know who was serious and who wasn't. The money was never worth my dignity.

Hook & Fasten engaged with companies that felt

they were ready to combat their anti-Blackness, when the truth is: Many of them weren't. While some slipped through the cracks, I refused to work with places that participated in the same type of work environments that did their best to ruin Black people and keep us in a lower position of equity and power.

Four years into my business, I'm still talking myself out of it and sometimes, I still allow the voice of limitations to creep into my head, telling me that this is the best it's going to get, leaving me ready to exit stage left as soon as a different challenge or opportunity comes up. I still have a hard time embracing what is good without waiting for the other shoe to drop. But what we must realize in these moments is that if we're always looking for the other shoe, we're not able to be present in what *is*—for me, this amazing company I created that serves the community in a sustainable and unique way that puts power, resources, and finances in the hands of people who need it. I make partnerships come to life that center people, just like I used to before and during my time in the White House. Just like I've always wanted to. My no-bullshit attitude was birthed in Philly. It's who I've always been and it's what helped me to get by, to be real, and to run a successful business.

Still I must remind myself: *This place is not familiar. I have not been here before.*

CHAPTER 10

Survival Is Fluid

Five years after leaving the White House, six years into a deeply intense healing regimen, and two years after starting a successful impact firm, I sat poolside in Florida basking in the sun. It was March and although it was slightly chilly, anything beat the cold winter waiting for me back up North. Wes and I had moved to Washington, DC, during the pandemic. Overall, I was feeling pretty good about life. I was wedding planning and in the midst of it, a recruiting firm reached out to me about an open position at a dream company. I wasn't particularly looking to close down Hook & Fasten, but I hadn't quite been sold on the entrepreneur life and was keeping my options open. I had multiple interviews with this company, and they generally liked me, I think—and I generally liked them. I was overly confident in a way that felt strange to me. I made peace with all the earlier versions of me while loving the present version of me and feeling good about the future versions of me. I was walking on what felt like sunshine every day.

This was also the first time since I'd left the White House that I'd gone through a hiring process with multiple interviews and negotiations. I was so excited that all my morning rituals, therapy sessions, self-care practices, and personal development around being a Black woman had yielded a cleansing of my soul, allowing me to understand the meaning and purpose of joy. I was taking each day as it came, careful not to fall into a pattern of *not* enjoying the present because I was too busy being highly anxious about the hypothetical upcoming doom moments. My evolution was still in motion, but in these moments, it felt like I'd tamed the beast of imposter syndrome and oh, it felt so good.

We were in Florida visiting Wes's aunt and uncle, who were snowbirds, alternating their time between Vermont and Florida. This was our second trip there as a couple and escaping the frigid winter, if only for one weekend, was a highlight we looked forward to. I was well adjusted to working wherever I was, and taking an actual vacation when you work for yourself is a lot harder than it seems, at least in the first year or two. I had employees, but I was the face of Hook & Fasten and held the most institutional knowledge and experience of effective impact. At least I had control of my schedule and opted to leave the mornings open for my self-care routine, walks and breakfast with Wes. On this particular day, I woke up full of excitement and vigor because my first meeting of the day, at noon, was with the recruiter for this job I'd been interviewing for.

This job would give me a chance to continue the line of working for powerful, philanthropic leaders who were dedicated to equality, fairness, and justice. I had plans to use the money from this job to go back to school, to learn the financial logistics of giving and sustainability. I would also be able to move to California, feeding my wanderlust for living on the West Coast for a few years. I was so excited. All the pieces were lining up, or so I thought. As the clock counted down to noon, I rushed into the vacation apartment on the bottom floor of the tall condo building that sat on the beach. I grabbed my notebook so I could be sure to write down details of the offer to review later on, once the excitement and celebration had quieted down. I was well qualified for this role, and my personality, prestige, and experience seemed to match the team that I'd be joining. I got comfy on the pastel couch, dialed the recruiter, and bit the cap off my black ballpoint pen, anxious at what was to come. The recruiter, Janet, had just come off vacation and this was her first day back.

"Hi. How was your vacation?"

"It was wonderful and nice to go visit my family."

"That's good to hear."

Her tone was off a bit. Like someone who wasn't excited to be on the phone. Surely making someone an offer was good news; why did she sound so down? Maybe it was the return to work? Maybe she had jet lag?

Maybe her luggage got lost? I've often been in a state of sadness after a vacation, so I totally got it. But also, wasn't she due to make a good chunk of change off my hire? These recruiters make bank; she should be happy. I would be! She proceeded to talk. Here it comes!!

"Unfortunately, I talked to the client, and they've decided to go with another candidate. They told me it was a hard decision, but ultimately the other candidate had more managerial experience with large teams. We'll keep you in mind for future opportunities."

She was quick and brash, cold and unemotional, which I didn't blame her for—that's the job, I guess.

"Thank you for letting me know and for helping throughout the process. Have a great day."

The next few minutes happened in slow motion. I quickly hung up the phone in utter disbelief. The time was 12:04 p.m. Four minutes. It took just four minutes for everything I had worked on to be tested with an unexpected rejection. I sat in silence looking at a blank piece of paper that had the company name and date on it, and nothing underneath. My thoughts were racing. Wes was still at the pool, giving me privacy on the call, but already amped up to celebrate. My body just sat on the couch frozen, unable to process what I'd just heard. I went to text Wes to tell him the call was over, but my fingers couldn't even move.

This sounds hella dramatic, I know. People get told no all the time about job opportunities, but this was more than that. This felt like I'd betrayed myself by having too much confidence. I'd become what I was always afraid of: cocky and conceited. I'd been in imposter syndrome rehab for years and was on the verge of relapse with just one phone call.

This wasn't the end of the world at all, but I allowed myself to be honest and say it really sucked and I took myself back to a place of fear, one of lack and blame. Scared that I'd start to constantly think thoughts of doubt, scared that I was relying on my ability and accolades to define my worth, and scared that I'd be running from this forever. I started to replay the interviews over in my head, dissecting every little bit where it could have gone wrong, where I might have gone wrong.

This moment was pivotal for me. It was one in which I had to make a quick decision of whether to shake off this disappointment or give in to it. I wasn't sure how to hold both or live in between. I could already feel my shoulders creeping up at the painful taste of defeat. I could already hear the voices that followed me from childhood and throughout my White House career starting to get louder. They would bring up everything I'd felt in my forty-three years about being a Black girl who was "lucky" to dodge circumstances that would have otherwise killed me. The voices reminded me of my "luck" in obtaining all the good things that happened in my life after the White House—the Harvard fellowship, finding my life partner, and starting my business. They yelled louder and *louder* trying to drown out feelings that I'd *earned* and deserved every bit of. But nah, I wasn't going down that road. Fuck that. Nope. I'd come too far and, to be honest, while imposter syndrome was a familiar feeling for me, there was something else rising up in my body that repelled, rejected, and fought it off, reminding me that we live in a world that thrives off Black women feeling inferior—a feeling that snuck inside my being when I was young and immature, planting that seed that would infest the most important parts of my life and attack my foundation of self. These feelings of inferiority get passed down generation after generation, creating a cycle of Black women who are pitted against the good parts of themselves for the sake of approval from those clamoring to remain in power.

I know I have to eventually leave this couch, I thought. It was twenty minutes since I'd hung up the phone, but my anger was quickly overpowering my disappointment, leaving me engulfed with rage and confusion. I had flashbacks to the many times that I'd heard the same sentiments of unworthiness being repeated to me from Black women, especially those who are young. Instead of existing in our wholeness, we critique our imperfections. We have developed a numbness that gives permission for pain and struggle to thrive within us. The smiles we carry are mere fronts that disguise our cries for rest, love, affirmation, and tenderness. I deserve leisurely walks in spaces of joy, though I also make mistakes and fail—and that is okay because all of it makes up who I am. Who we are. This beautiful, complicated creature of contradictions, revelations, and evolution. *Yes, yes...let's go with that*, I thought, *because this sunken place of despair at the hands of others is not it.* It'll never be it for me or for us again.

I texted Wes that I was done with the phone call and would come out to the pool to let him know what happened. I stood up with the vigor of someone who was ready to run a marathon. My legs were strong, holding up the rest of my body with confidence. I didn't feel ashamed or bad about not getting this dream job. I had to trust that I might never find out why I didn't get it but took root in the fact that it wasn't something I should attack myself over, either.

Slipping on my flip-flops, I walked out to my chair at the pool as Wes emerged from the water, dried off, and sat next to me. He put his cold hand on my leg and saw in my face that it wasn't the best news. I casually blurted out, "Nope, didn't get it. Sucks, but such is life." I didn't even recognize myself while saying that. Who was this woman now so detached from a statement that was so devastating just forty-five minutes ago? Perhaps I was coping by detachment? Nah, this was definitely something else.

After we hugged for a second, Wes got dressed and we strolled down the street to a restaurant for some food and libations. I wasn't trying to mess up a whole day because of this, really. It still stung, no doubt, but I was moving on.

In practicality, how exactly do you just move on from situations that challenge your core, situations that have you questioning who you are? I get asked this so very often when I speak about imposter syndrome, when I teach and when I mentor. The answer is: I have no choice but to keep going, reminding myself that imposter syndrome is an oppressive term and feeling working as designed.

The term *survival* is fluid in its application, depending on its context and use. Often it is used as a positive, a strength, a badge of honor, a symbol of triumph, a descriptor of someone who has lived through struggle and has come out on the other side. It's a relatable identifier that many of us have subscribed to. But survival can also be viewed as a tactic of last resort and desperation, an act of hanging on at all costs. For many with imposter syndrome, it's the latter more than the former.

Even when surrounded with unconditional love and support from others who lift you up and fill in the gaps for you when you can't take those steps ahead yourself, survival often comes down to your well-being, which we as individuals are ultimately responsible for. Systems, and those controlling those systems, thrive off holding the remote control to how *we* perceive *ourselves* and what we *believe* about ourselves. It's all so hard to be in the thick of a battle you aren't quite sure you'll come out of. I've been there in those moments, clenching my teeth, counting down until the hard days and hard times are over—when I can finally open my eyes again and not be scared of what's ahead. It's in those moments that I feel the most helpless and hopeless, unaware of my next movements and steps, cursing God for abandoning me. It's really an all-around mind fuck, if I'm being honest. And I know that most of us have felt this way at one time or another. Maybe more often than we care to relive.

As I live and breathe, I promise you that there's a way out of these swirling thoughts, feelings, and emotions. THERE IS A WAY OUT! The advice I've given is what worked for me. You will find what works for you, but please use these words and my story as a blueprint for knowing you should be wholly loved, wholly appreciated, and wholly valued in your truest form. Use the power that is nestled within your anger and sadness to draw the boundary of *no. No* to treating yourself like shit, thinking you ain't shit, or letting people talk to you like shit. I took the test. I am your testimony.

As mentioned, it will feel so odd and strange when you first establish this boundary of *no.* Imposter syndrome will turn its back on you, try to make you feel like you're being mean or selfish. *Don't* fall for it. Don't you dare feel guilty. You are finally putting *yourself* first. This is what it feels like.

You may find, sadly, that this may cause a separation between you and the people in your life, because putting yourself first causes you to change your environment and your mind in order to seek a renewed love of self. Not everyone will like or appreciate that you're finally taking care of yourself. There will be those, you'll find out, who will resent you for taking a stand. But did those people ever really have your best interest at heart in the first place if they can't stand to see you happy and taking care of yourself mentally and emotionally? Or were they only comfortable being there for you when your doubt was used for their power? Ask yourself that.

We have to show others how to treat us, and we do so by first treating ourselves with the same dignity, compassion, respect, and affirmation that we used to seek from others. This is your permission slip to walk with your shoulders down with resolution and chin up with confidence, one foot in front of the other.

You've been shouldering around the weight of doubt too long. Put it down, it's not yours to carry anymore.

ACKNOWLEDGMENTS

God, you are the author and architect. For the grace and mercy you continue to show me, I will forever credit any victories to you. In the beginning and the end, this is for your glory and my lips will always repeat a magnitude of thank-yous until I can no more.

After that, I lose my way swimming in a sea of people to thank because so many have touched me along the way that it's nearly impossible to remember. I'm hoping that the right people know the beautiful space they hold in my life, even if not mentioned by name below.

To those reading these words from an unsafe space, a questioning space, a confused space, know you are valued, needed, and loved. Give yourself grace, speak to yourself with compassion. I don't know you but I love you!

Dyer Family, for giving me life (parents Dianna and Isaac Jr.), continued support, encouragement, and for sticking it out through it all, I thank you. Specifically my first friend, my brother Isaac III and his wife, Desiree, and kids, Justice, Jasmyne, and Isaac IV. Extended family (including Uncle Rick…can we get over the wedding invite now?), hoping the future brings us together more. Continue to walk in greatness. Love you all!

Kerri Fogus, Taylor Fogus, Marie Dixon, and broader family, there will never be enough words or enough love to convey how much I have appreciated having you in my life for nearly thirty years. Kerri, you are forever my soulmate, my best friend, and the keeper of all secrets.

Angel Ramirez and Amaya Rawls, for all the talks, walks, laughs, and memories built over thirty-six years. Oh and the rice, let's not forget the rice. My wish for you both is that you always see yourselves as valued, loved, beautiful, and worthy as I see you.

Brandon Lepow, I miss you. You would be front-row and center at my book events. The impact you left on this earth and on me is unmeasurable.

Mr. Lewis Webster, thank you for being the best teacher, counselor, and advocate to all students at Milton Hershey School. It meant everything to have you and Mrs. Eula Webster in the classroom growing up, the only two Black teachers I've ever had. We miss your wise counsel, big smile, and corny jokes.

Leslie Jordan, you are missed and you are loved. Your trust and belief in me will always be something I am thankful to the heavens for. I just know you are giggling and singing somewhere.

The village of friends and framily that have held me in all the ebbs and flows. You are a special community of healers, lovers, dreamers, and doers that inspire and feed my soul and belly. You all have stuck with me through so many years and transitions.

President Barack and Mrs. Michelle Obama, you laid the foundation for so many of us to think beyond what was possible for ourselves. Thank you for choosing and TRUSTING a rough-around-the-edges girl to represent you. White House colleagues, you believed in me enough to be your peer, especially Patrick Whitty, who made that intern phone call, and Alyssa Mastromonaco, who offered me the job.

Former interns, mentees, employees, sometimes you didn't get the best version of me as a leader, boss, or mentor as I figured myself out. I'm deeply sorry but know that I'm always going to stand ten toes down for all y'all.

Dr. Mary Conway and the Community College of Philadelphia, you gave me a chance when other colleges wouldn't. It was because of your care for students and for me that I ended up at the White House.

Julie and Randy Mladenoff, my first home at Milton Hershey School and those good memories of us dancing, doing gymnastics, and twirling batons are my most treasured times.

Hook & Fasten team past and present, thank you for holding me down during this process and several years of business.

beGirl.world Global Scholars girls and team, we are always the little engine that could. One day the world will catch up...or not? Either way, we will keep it moving. Faith without works?! HA!

All my therapists, you definitely earned them fees!

Sheesh. I wouldn't have made it through this process or this life without your care and safety.

Ashley C. Ford, Ruthie Mae Bolton, Tarana Burke, and bell hooks, you all wrote books that made me understand it was okay to be vulnerable. Your books comforted me and healed me. I've read a lot, but your books changed me in ways I'm still digesting.

Kellie McGann, Felice Laverne, you helped me move my words over some very large mountains when doubt stepped in.

Legacy Lit team, especially Krishan Trotman and Amina Iro. Your patience and guidance are worth gold and I'm so thankful that you invested in this project and in me. Always stand firm, tall, and proud in the power you hold to tell our stories.

Park & Fine Literary Media, we did it! Sarah Passick, you are beyond the best. You pushed me to expect and demand more, a lesson that will stick with me far beyond this book. Emily Sweet, John Maas, and Mia Vitale, your involvement, experience, and attention made such a difference. From random texts to my meltdowns, you all never let me feel a burden or bother...even if sometimes I was.

To all of you who picked up a call, answered a text, responded to an email, or just allowed me to use your shoulder and arms for comfort, advice, and love during this book writing process. I will always do the same in return.

Wes Moe, we have shared our life with sixty thousand words for nearly two years. For the love you give when this art commands me to become someone you don't immediately recognize, I am grateful. Thanks

for loving me but thanks even more for liking me. Let's keep dancing on the 2's and 4's, shall we?

To YOU, yes YOU—the reader! Thank you for walking beside me gently and carefully.

Lastly, I also want to acknowledge the authors who have come before me and the ones who will come after, especially Black women. We are the sun, the moon, and all things in between. Thank you for holding me accountable to my greatness and growth. You showed me that I can't be like you as much as I wanted to. I had to discover my writing voice, my art, my creativity. You have toiled in the soil, so I can harvest the crop. I honor you by continuing on with this body of work and future literary bodies of work.

In joy and truth, always.

...okay, that wasn't brief, but I'm a writer. I tried!